The PIE LADY

"I'm grateful that this book exists. Mennonite foodways are about more than food; they're connections to family, faith, and history. These stories bring the people behind the recipes to life, alongside many tasty and comforting dishes."
—*Hannah Faith Notess, author of* The Multitude

"Why merely make a pie when you could make a pie and a story at the same time? In *The Pie Lady*, Greta Isaac does exactly that, weaving simple stories of simple lives with the mouthwatering recipes of the women who lived them. She has a gift for making everyday things beautiful and showcasing the love of ordinary women. After all, if all it takes to make you happy is 'a pink petunia or a perfect loaf of bread—then it's easy to be rich and happy, and the world belongs to you.' I am a storyteller, not a cook, but after reading this book, I wanted to go out to the kitchen and start mixing. Every recipe in it is meaningful because every recipe has a story."
—*Lucinda J. Miller, author of* Anything but Simple

The PIE LADY

*Classic Stories from a Mennonite
Cook and Her Friends*

GRETA ISAAC

HERALD
P R E S S

Harrisonburg, Virginia

Herald Press
PO Box 866, Harrisonburg, Virginia 22803
www.HeraldPress.com

Library of Congress Cataloging-in-Publication Data
Names: Isaac, Greta, author.
Title: The pie lady : classic stories from a Mennonite cook and her friends /
    Greta Isaac.
Other titles: Classic stories from a Mennonite cook and her friends
Description: Harrisonburg : Herald Press, [2019] | Series: Plainspoken :
    real-life stories of Amish and Mennonites
Identifiers: LCCN 2018049719 | ISBN 9781513804217 (pbk. : alk. paper)
Subjects: LCSH: Mennonites—United States—Social life and customs. |
    Mennonite women—Ancedotes. | Mennonite cooking.
Classification: LCC E184.M45 I83 2019 | DDC 289.7/73—dc23 LC record
    available at https://lccn.loc.gov/2018049719

THE PIE LADY
© 2019 by Herald Press, Harrisonburg, Virginia 22803. 800-245-7894.
    All rights reserved.
Library of Congress Control Number: 2018049719
International Standard Book Number: 978-1-5138-0421-7 (paperback);
    978-1-5138-0423-1 (ebook)
Printed in United States of America
Cover and interior design by Merrill Miller
Cover photo by Hope Helmuth

Unless otherwise noted, Scripture text is quoted from The Holy Bible, King
James Version.

23 22 21 20 19   10 9 8 7 6 5 4 3 2 1

To my family and friends
and the friends of my friends:
All you wonderful Pie Ladies.

CONTENTS

INTRODUCTION TO

PLⲆINSPOKEN
Real-life stories of Amish and Mennonites

NOVELS, TOURIST SITES, and television shows offer second- or third-hand accounts of Amish, Mennonite, and Hutterite life. Some of these messages are sensitive and accurate. Some are not. Many are flat-out wrong.

Now readers can listen directly to the voices of these Anabaptists themselves through Plainspoken: Real-Life Stories of Amish and Mennonites. In the books in this series, readers get to hear Amish, Mennonite, and Hutterite writers talk about the texture of their daily lives: how they spend their time, what they value, what makes them laugh, and how they summon strength from their Christian faith and community.

Plain Anabaptists are publishing their writing more than ever before. But this literature is read mostly by other Amish, Mennonites, and Hutterites, and rarely by the larger reading public.

Through Plainspoken, readers outside their communities can learn what authentic Plain Anabaptist life looks and feels like—from the inside out. The Amish and Mennonites and Hutterites have stories to tell. Through Plainspoken, readers get the chance to hear them.

Author's Note

*And that ye study to be quiet, and to do your own
business, and to work with your own hands.*

—1 THESSALONIANS 4:11

*There is nothing better for a man, than that he should eat
and drink, and that he should make his soul enjoy good
in his labour. This also I saw, that it was from
the hand of God.*

—ECCLESIASTES 2:24

THIS IS JUST to say—

Thank you.

Thank you to Matt and our children, my mom and my sisters, my family and friends. Thanks for each hour we have shared in the kitchen and at the table.

Thank you to the friends I write with.

And thank you especially to each friend who shared a Pie Lady story with me. There would be no book without you. Each of these stories is true. In each story, I tried to write enough to give you a picture of a life. Some of the stories are about people

I know well, and others are stories people sent to me. For those stories, they sent me the recipe and several pages of memories. Then I wrote it into a story and sent it back. They corrected me wherever I had details wrong, and we kept going until it sounded right. So it's their stories and their recipes—your stories and your recipes—all across the United States and Canada.

It's only the tiniest piece of what could be said. There could be a whole book written about any of these cooks, or about any one of you. Each life is so amazing and so full. I have loved hearing the details of so many lives. I loved the opportunity to spend time thinking of all us women, thousands of miles away or just around the corner, doing our own quiet work on ordinary days and suddenly finding—in a pie, in a casserole, in a pan of gravy—a glamorous, glittery Pie Lady moment.

Yes.

Whether or not your story is in this book, it's about you, of course, in the small square on this earth that you call home.

1

The Pie Lady

ERMA

A merry heart doeth good like a medicine.

—PROVERBS 17:22

ERMA MARRIED JAKE when she was twenty-four years old. She had planned to become a nurse and had already started her nurse's training. But those were the old days, when you could not take nurse's training if you were a married woman. So Erma changed her plans and married Jake. Jake had a farm and a dairy, and Erma looked forward to the life ahead of them.

She jumped right in to married life. Their first house wasn't finished, but that didn't bother Erma. She set up a board, with a couple of dishpans across it, and had a counter. She stretched a curtain across the board and had a cupboard.

Life rolled by. Children came, and much more work. Harvesttime came, and planting season. Milking time came around every day. She was tired and busy. There were long days, long hours, multiple responsibilities. It took everything she had, day after day.

There were moments, though! Moments when cream puffs really did puff up high in the oven. Moments when she walked into the girls' room, singing them awake. Bright moments in a life of work, late and early. The children packed around the table for suppers of chocolate pudding (no eggs in it at suppertime—you don't want it too rich), fried potatoes, dill pickles, and buttered bread. They worked hard, but Erma took time to teach them all to sing. She sang song after song, old-fashioned songs, taught them to sing up and down the scale until they learned all the notes.

Jake loved cows, but he never loved the dairy. Milking was such a constant thing. After twenty-five years of dairy life, Jake and Erma moved to Texas, where he could ranch and farm. There the cattle grazed the fields. Jake took them out to a ranch for the summers and brought them home in the winter. It was a long drive out to the ranch over empty, grassy hills, a perfect drive for a cattleman.

Erma drew plans for a new house, a ranch-style house in Texas. They moved into a house in the small Texas town and started building the house out on the farm. She had never liked unfinished basements, so they framed up the house and closed it in, and then finished the basement first. It took years for them to save up enough money to finish the upstairs part of the house, and they spent years living in that basement. She kept at it, though, year after year—so with the basement house, and then the upstairs one, Erma had a new house twice.

She loved it. She did a lot of the wiring herself, and the painting and the staining and who knows what else. And quite a lot of it she paid for with her pie money.

Because my grandma Erma was a Pie Lady. I used to spend a week or so there in Texas during summers, and oh, the work we did and the pies I watched her make! I got out of bed early, those pie-baking days. Her hands flew, the stove was filled with kettles, and somehow she stirred continuously, all those kettles at once.

We slipped those pies into perfect pie boxes, stacked them carefully onto specially made racks in the trunk of her car, and took them to the local café. There people sprang to open the door and to open the fridge: "Here's the Pie Lady!"

It was fun. It made the morning—and that endless stack of dishes—worthwhile. I was tall, those mornings. I carried the boxes carefully. After all, I was with the Pie Lady.

There were other worthwhile things about those early morning town trips, and one of the best was the Ben Franklin store. Grandma took us there every year to get a piece of fabric. We got to choose our very own piece. Then she would sew it into a dress for us or help us to sew it on our own.

One year she taught us to make doll dresses. She found a pattern in the *Childcraft* magazine and adapted it to include sleeves, short or long. We've used that pattern, and handed it out to other little girls, year after year.

Whatever she had in front of her, Erma was ready. She took her life and filled it up. Make a counter, a cupboard, a new yard, a new house. Jump up on the table, swat a fly on the ceiling. Work hard, do what it takes so things are done the way you want them done—and then hurry off and make a pie.

Years later, in the middle of an accomplishing sort of day (I only have them occasionally), I felt like Grandma, and suddenly I realized something: Erma was not working for the goal but the doing. Pioneering—and even the simple doing of things—can feel rewarding, fulfilling. You take flour and shortening and have a grand creation. You take a grimy, messy spot and make a quiet place to relax. You take an empty plot of native grass and make a home. On a Pie Lady day, there's a good chance you will feel like packing up a picnic and running off to the lake for supper. Why not? Life is good, every moment—and we can do a lot to build something lovely out of it.

Erma really was a builder. She built for fun too. Most of our growing-up years, their upstairs was a fun place of unfinished rooms. In the back corner, Grandma made us girls a three-room playhouse, complete with a clothes rack and small wire hangers. We spent hours in that playhouse, planning and cooking and tending dolls. It was fun, except—always—there was a chance that some huge tall cousins would come in, stomping up the stairs to our house to scare us. We rocked and cooked with our ears open.

One summer Grandma made a birthday cake house. She made a cake in an 8 x 8-inch pan and cut and frosted it, complete with a triangle roof and a chimney. And then she loaded us into the car and drove around the neighborhood, inviting girls over for a birthday party.

We will never forget Grandma's perfectly baked ham or her Thanksgiving turkey. She had her little tricks—save netting from grapes to separate the turkey from the dressing—and she worked all hours, getting it right. She wrote out a turkey roast recipe for us, and it tells you to put it in about midnight. It also tells you what to do with it at six in the morning. She told us how to can fruit using a pressure canner, how to make pork fingers (use tenderized pork, cut it in strips, roll it in flour with plenty of seasoned salt, fry in hot oil), how to make fun things like peach pit jelly or fried apples.

Erma planted trees and made a yard. She grew roses and geraniums. She sewed quilt tops and quilted them, one after another. And every summer, Grandma took us out to the lake for a picnic dinner. She always took her homemade hamburger buns and we grilled hamburgers, and we always had cantaloupe. We hiked back around the lake and saw the dinosaur tracks in the rocks. We went out on the lake in our uncle's canoe. And then we went home and drank sweet tea. We opened the fridge and got a jar of her tea brew, dumped a cup of it into her clear pink pitcher, and added water. Then we filled our cups with ice and sat down and enjoyed it.

Life can be full of Pie Lady moments—of course it can. A Pie Lady moment is Erma bending down to watch the cream puffs in the oven: "Come and see!" It's lifting golden squash rings to a bright serving platter, serving breakfast on the patio, or making a long-awaited turkey casserole. It's a moment of goodness or glamour in an ordinary day.

Maybe I can do a Pie Lady thing today, just today: enjoy the doing, maybe even a great tall stack of it. Maybe I can find the thing I can do, the thing I can make with my own two hands, whatever my thing is. Maybe I can pack up a picnic for a trip to the lake. Maybe I can plan a house or start a yard. Or maybe I can just make a pie.

Here is Erma's pie crust recipe and her no-fail cooked meringue. There's nothing quite like pie crust: the white flour, soft and mounded in the bowl; the exact measurement of salt, fine and white against the flour; the cutting of the shortening until the crumbs are moist; the pile of crumbs up into a hill;

the well you dip into the crumbs and the careful tablespoons of ice water you pour into it; the mixing and rolling and pinching and pricking and baking. It's all a great way to feel that you did something extra, and it hardly matters if it turns out perfectly or not. From all those white ingredients—flour, salt, ice, and shortening—you get a golden, crispy thing. Any pudding or custard filling will do it good, any fruity, sugary mix will feel at home in it, and any person big or little will be glad to meet it.

Oh, and the meringue! It really is fun to watch it whip, to stop the mixer and stick in your spoon and pull it up and see if you can make pretty peaks. And then if you do get it right, and you swoop the piled-up stuff into lovely droopy peaks, you smile and feel like this was a day worth marking. You set the pie on the lowest shelf in the oven and watch it brown, and if there's a little person anywhere nearby, you let them peek. Otherwise you peek yourself, once in a while, and you maybe even grin at that mountainy thing.

Good times do us good.

PIE CRUST

> 2 cups flour
> 1 teaspoon salt
> ⅔ cup plus 2 tablespoons shortening
> About 4 tablespoons ice water

Preheat oven to 350°F. Mix flour and salt. Cut in shortening. Make a well in your crumbs and add ice water. Mix with fork just until it sticks together. Form into two balls. Press each one into a round disc. Roll out on a floured counter and place in 9-inch pie pans. If you are making a cream pie, prick with fork across the bottom and around the sides. Bake 25 minutes. Or freeze the unbaked pie shell and bake when you are ready to fill it. Just put the frozen shell in the oven and bake it for 25 minutes.

MERINGUE

3 egg whites
3 tablespoons granulated sugar
1 tablespoon cornstarch
⅛ teaspoon salt
⅓ cup plus 1 tablespoon water
¼ teaspoon vanilla extract
⅛ heaping teaspoon cream of tartar

Preheat oven to 350°F. Place egg whites in a bowl and set within a bowl of warm water so that egg whites will be a bit warmer than room temperature. Combine sugar, cornstarch, salt, and water in a small saucepan. Bring to a boil, stirring constantly. Boil just a bit, then remove from heat and add vanilla. Set in fridge or cool water to cool to room temperature.

Combine egg whites and cream of tartar and beat just until the egg whites start to peak. Add your cooled-off sugar mixture. Beat just until it makes nice peaks. Pile meringue on top of warm pie filling, going clear to the crust to seal the edges. Swoop your spoon through the meringue to make peaks. Bake on lowest shelf of oven, 15–20 minutes.

2

Something Different

JULIA

At thy right hand there are pleasures for evermore.

—PSALM 16:11

JULIA WAS NOT a Pie Lady. Oh, she could make a pie if she wanted to. In fact, she knew her pie crust recipe by heart. But Julia was more often in search of something new, something different. Some of the different things turned into family traditions—but not all of them, of course. That's how new things are.

Julia knew all about pleasures, about blessings, about the joy of the church she chose. She loved her family, and she knew that sparkly things—Pie Lady moments—could be found all over the place. Life held many changes for her, one after another. Julia was twenty-one when she joined her sister's Mennonite church, and she was still twenty-one when she married Sam. Julia loved her new home. She loved her new life with Sam.

Sam and Julia had not been married long when World War II broke out and Sam was called up for military service. Sam felt he could not serve in the war because he believed that we should "resist not evil" (Matthew 5:39). The government granted Sam the status of a conscientious objector and gave him work to do for the country in place of military service.

Julia stayed home in Kansas until Steven, their first baby, was born. After several months, she moved to Colorado to be near Sam. She found a place where she could work as house help while she took care of Steven. Julia loved working there, loved learning how to set a beautiful table, loved caring for beautiful things. And Sam biked over on the weekends to be with Julia and Steven. Those were the best evenings in the quiet kitchen, where the three of them could have a few special hours.

But Steven was not well, and he got sicker instead of better. He was only three years old when he went to heaven.

Sam and Julia never talked about Steven without tears. He was their own first baby, and the daughter and the five sons who came later of course never completely filled his place. But life was good, life was full. Sam was a preacher now, and there were many obligations that went along with that, many things to think about and remember. The house filled up with people, with talk and laughter. They all loved to tell stories and laugh over them. They spent hours singing together. When one of the boys wrote his own song, Julia added the alto line.

The work went on, the years went by. The children grew up, married, and made lives of their own. And always, Julia found bright and beautiful things. She loved coffee breaks, and time to talk or read in the living room. She loved auctions and garage sales and dinner in town. She could get enthused about a heated-up frozen dinner or a table set with the prettiest dishes.

All her life, she loved to set the table the way she had learned at the housekeeping job she had when she was a young mom. She loved to learn to make something new and serve it on a red tablecloth. Friends from India taught her to make chicken curry, and she made it for special occasions, each topping served in special lovely dishes. When you piled the curry on your plate, you wanted to use every single topping—it made the most delightful contrast of flavors.

To make chicken curry, you cook a whole chicken with onions and curry until the chicken is tender and falling off the bones. Then you debone the chicken, thicken the broth, and return the chicken to it. You serve it over hot white rice and top it with toppings, each of them in a beautiful little bowl set on a red cloth: bananas, tomatoes, raisins, green onions, coconut, lettuce, pineapple, and salted peanuts.

Have you ever realized that things can make you happy? They can, of course—they should. You can pour coconut into a red dish and smile over it. You can find the very bowl you'd been looking for at the latest auction. You can stop along the road to watch a prairie dog town. You can pack up your suitcase a week before you leave on a trip, adding things as you think of them, enjoying and stretching out that exciting getting-ready part of your trip. Life may not be perfect, but it's full of lovely things.

My grandma Julia took each of us grandchildren on drives to local antique shops. We would go out for breakfast at the local Mexican restaurant before school. Grandma bought us things, small things that were thoughtful and special. Once when she visited her family in California, she came home with three bantam Silkie chicks, which have soft feathers that feel almost like hair. She had put those three tiny chickens in their box on her lap on the plane, all the way from California to Kansas. Grandma walked straight, facing life with a smile. We felt taller, those days, walking beside her.

Julia had her favorite recipes and even her secret recipes. My sisters and I spent hours with her when Christmas was getting close, rolling peppernuts and her soft, special, sugary Russian Rocks. We drank pop out of teacups for our "midnight snack." We laughed while she told us stories of growing up, of playing softball with the boys.

"The first time I was up to bat, they all moved in," Grandma said. She grinned. "The next time, they all moved out."

We laughed and wished we could play ball like Grandma had. And then we settled down with books to read, on the couch under the chime clock.

By that time, my grandpa Sam was blind.

He and Julia had planned their retirement, the trips they would take and the things they would do. He was sixty-five, and almost there, when he went out to work early one morning. He reached the corner in his car at just the same time as his friend from town. The friend had a stop sign, but he looked down the open road and it looked empty. He didn't see Sam.

After the accident, Sam was blind and partially paralyzed. After he got well again, he and Julia spent a lot of time together. It was not the retirement that they had pictured, but you can guarantee that they always had time for the grandchildren, for suppers and talks and overnights. They always had time to fill the candy cupboard and the shelf of pop in the fridge.

Not so many years later, Julia started having symptoms of Alzheimer's. We'd pull up to their house for supper, Dad and Mom and five small- and medium-sized children, and she'd meet us at the door, laughing with the joy of seeing us: "I thought we'd have something different for supper!" she'd say. Then, many times over those days, we'd have the same "different" menu—waffles, crisp and golden brown, with fried sausages and perfect brown sugar syrup.

Years later, after Grandma was gone, I learned that there is a trick to making that syrup. I knew that she always made it with half-and-half instead of regular cream, and I knew it was thick and rich. But whenever I'd try to make it, it would turn out lumpy or thin, or strange, somehow.

"Oh yes," my mother-in-law told me when I told her about the syrup attempts. "You cannot let it boil. You use equal amounts of half-and-half and brown sugar, and you stir it pretty constantly until it is warm, and then it is done."

Things like that—and like those perfect, no-recipe waffles— Julia remembered. I hope I am the same—that I remember good, rich things when lesser things have failed me.

One day before the waffle days, Grandma and I sorted recipes at her kitchen table. I had received a recipe folder for Christmas, and Grandma was ready to help me try to fill it up. She pulled out magazine clippings and handwritten pages, looked them over, and set them down. Every now and then she pulled one out. "You've got to copy this one," she said.

I copied them, one after another, and stuck them in my book. She copied some too. And I tried them, and used them, one after another. One day a few years ago, I was turning through that book and found a recipe I had never paid much attention to, a recipe she copied down for me that day. Apparently we had run out of recipe cards, because this was on a small lined paper, just the kind I remembered her using in a little black book she took to church to write sermon notes in. The recipe was for sugar cookies.

I wondered why she gave this one to me. Most of her recipes were something unusual, a recipe from India, a topping for a pumpkin pie, gumdrop cookies, a salad you make by tearing everything with your hands. But this! It was called only Sugar Cookies.

I read the recipe over and wondered if she had copied it correctly: there were no eggs in these cookies. I tried it, and decided she was correct. They are so old-fashioned looking, so pretty and dependable, that I've made them over and over. I rarely grease cookie sheets, because I don't want the cookies to run—it's not usually necessary. But if you don't grease the cookie sheets on these, be sure you loosen them right away or they will tear when you take them off.

I'll give you her pumpkin pie topping recipe too—it's called "Out of This World," and it really is pretty special. It's also rich enough to be a rare treat.

There's a pretty plate in your cabinet. There's a treasure at the local auction. There's a perfect crispy waffle, a plate of old-fashioned cookies, a smiling welcome for someone coming in the door. Stand up straight, face life with a smile, spread the tablecloth, have a midnight snack.

It's time for something different.

SUGAR COOKIES

½ cup shortening
½ cup butter
½ cup granulated sugar, plus additional for dipping
½ cup brown sugar
1 teaspoon vanilla extract
1 teaspoon baking soda
½ teaspoon cream of tartar
½ teaspoon salt
2 cups flour
A few tablespoons cream, for dipping

Preheat oven to 350°F. Mix together shortening, butter, ½ cup granulated sugar, and brown sugar. Beat on medium speed of mixer at least 30 seconds, or until mixture is light and smooth. Mix in vanilla. Add baking soda, cream of tartar, salt, and flour. Mix on low speed just until blended.

Spoon out individual cookies. Dip in cream (Julia underlined the word *dip*. Only the tops, I guess—don't roll them in the topping!). Then dip in granulated sugar.

Bake 9–10 minutes, just until done. Loosen immediately, I will add.

"Use ice cream scoop to make cookies," Julia wrote. Maybe she made these cookies large, an ice cream scoop instead of a heaping teaspoon. I just use my cookie scoop. I love how soft they are, and I love the shiny tops.

OUT-OF-THIS-WORLD PUMPKIN PIE

¼ cup butter, melted
1 cup brown sugar
2 tablespoons light cream
1 cup chopped pecans
1 pumpkin pie, baked

Combine butter, brown sugar, cream, and pecans. Spread evenly over your baked pumpkin pie. Cover the edges of the pie with aluminum foil, and glaze under the broiler for 4–5 minutes. Stand and watch it broil—it just needs to bubble. It will brown a little, but you don't want this special pie to burn!

3

Delightful Dates and Other Details

CARISSA

But even the very hairs of your head are all numbered.

—LUKE 12:7

CARISSA'S FAMILY MOVED to our area one summer. I remember the excitement of it, remember wondering if it would be like a storybook in which a new girl moves in and becomes your friend. I remember our first visit at their house, out on the sandy Kansas hills. I remember the storybook fun of a brand-new friend.

Because it was storybook perfect, it really was. Carissa and I stood together on the bases during running games at recess. We laughed together over the balls we tried to throw. We sat together during art class and shared seventh-grade jokes. We did dishes at lunchtime, dusted desks on Wednesdays, and sat together in church on Sundays. We found God in the same set of revival meetings, learned to know the God who names the stars and numbers every hair on our heads.

We each had younger sisters. It was fun to know another big sister. It was fun to have someone to laugh with about being thirteen-year-olds who had to be Responsible Adults. As teenagers, we made biscuits for supper. (I ate some of the dough, I remember, and shocked Carissa. Raw eggs and everything, oh dear!) We decorated our canvas shoes with fabric pens, painted pictures on fabric, and sewed ourselves dresses. On a trip we took together after we were grown up enough to drive five hours alone, we stopped in to see her grandma. Then we dressed up in the old shoes and purses from her grandma's dress-up box and ran around the countryside meeting her aunts. The shoes and purses we were wearing had belonged to the aunts! Their favorite old shoes, that purse they thought was perfect! It was a funny day, and we ended it by going off to the volleyball game to play as little volleyball as possible. (It was the place where all the fun was, but neither of us played very well.)

Years later, as young moms, we made sloppy joes and invited a bunch of friends over to her in-law's big kitchen to make Christmas candy. ("What recipe did you use for the sloppy joes?" Carissa asked. "It was a mix," I admitted. "That's okay too," Carissa said.) We discussed cooking and canning and other responsible things. We rocked babies and did dishes. Now, as middle-aged moms, we meet for lunch and laugh to realize that we really *are* responsible adults. Now we can leave our daughters home to do responsible things.

When my brother died, Carissa and another friend came and cleaned our house. They left a poem on the table, carefully handwritten, with the edges of the paper torn just so. They used the alphabet letters on the fridge to write WE LOVE YOU. And they wiped the fridge clean before they wrote it.

It's details that make things sparkle: the perfectly sewn band around the neck on a new dress, the handmade pattern weights, the minutes grabbed for a visit with friends in the middle of a family holiday, the nutmeg in an apple pie. It's worth your time to make sure that the green tea is chilled, the grilled corn spiced, and the cornmeal rolls the softest ever. It pays off to keep every bean and eggplant in your garden patch watched and watered.

I wasn't surprised to see that Carissa had a pie recipe in a recent cookbook, or that the name of the pie is so pretty that you want to get acquainted. "It's a very mild flavor," Carissa said. "Those two fruits seem to really complement each other." It's worth making the pie just to see that bright, lovely pink, and just so you can write it on the chalkboard or the fridge: Rosy Raspberry Pear.

To make the pie, you slice 3 pears and toss them with 1 tablespoon lemon juice and ½ teaspoon almond extract. Then you add ¾ cup granulated sugar and 3 tablespoons flour and stir to coat. You spoon half the pears into an unbaked pie shell, add 1 cup raspberries, and top with the rest of your pears. You dot the whole thing with 1 or 2 tablespoons of butter and cover with a crust. Then you seal and crimp the pie crust edges, brush the top with 1 tablespoon melted margarine, and sprinkle it with 1 tablespoon granulated sugar. You bake the pie for 40 to 50 minutes at 400°F, and you serve it with ice cream. There it is, in the center of your table: Rosy Raspberry Pear.

Carissa sent me a recipe the other day, a family recipe from her mother-in-law. She remembers the day she walked into her mother-in-law's kitchen and saw a cereal-and-nut mixture in a pan on the counter. She remembers asking, "What's this?" She remembers the assurance that came from everyone at once, there in the kitchen: "It's really good."

Carissa helped to cut that mixture into small, perfect squares. Then she folded in the whipped cream and chose a dark red bowl. Into the red bowl she piled the sweet mixture for a date salad. It could be a dessert, of course. Maybe it should be a dessert, served in tall, stemmed jelly dishes. But this was Christmas, and that's a day when you can pick up the red dish of sweet stuff and call it a salad.

"Finger-licking-good!" Carissa decided. "Delightful!" Year after year, they made it again for special dinners—the sweet squares, the careful folding, the heap in the dark red bowl. Sometimes her mother-in-law kept a few of the chewy squares out and slipped them into a sack for the family's snack as they drove back home.

These days, Carissa makes the salad for her family, and when she serves it, she remembers those days in her mother-in-law's kitchen, tasting a sweet, chewy square, and then standing in front of the china cupboard searching for just the right bowl. She remembers the days they ate that salad: happy days, heartachy days, and all the days in between.

"It will always be a special recipe for Christmas," Carissa says. Of course it will, with the white piled high against the red, the squares you held back going home with the children.

We love you, delightful date! You definitely belong on the same table as Rosy Raspberry Pear.

Take care.

CHRISTMAS DATE SALAD

¾ cup granulated sugar
½ cup butter
1 egg, beaten
1 cup chopped dates
¾ cup chopped pecans
2 cups crispy rice cereal
12 ounces whipped cream

Bring sugar, butter, beaten egg, dates, and pecans to a boil over medium heat. Cook 5 minutes, stirring constantly. Remove from heat and stir in rice cereal. Pour into buttered 8 x 8-inch pan. Place in refrigerator to cool. Cut into 1-inch squares. Fold into whipped cream.

4

Carried Me Through

LOTTIE

As every man hath received the gift,
even so minister the same one to another.

—1 PETER 4:10

HARVEY AND LOTTIE turned onto the last road on their long journey. It was a rough road with no pavement, and a new home was at the end of it.

It wasn't a home like their Michigan home, not at all. It was gray and unpainted and small, this Georgia house, huddled there behind the pecan tree. Harvey and Lottie had a family of nine to move into it. Lottie cried at the sight of it, just as she had cried all along that long, long road.

Gnats were everywhere, and you had to bat them away from your face. ("These are the friendliest people ever," the story ran. "They're always waving.")

Still, it was home. Home! Lottie dried her tears and buttoned up her lip. She set up beds for the family, swept the wide-board floor. She opened the flour bin in the cupboard, and she started baking.

And how she baked! Bread and cookies and pies and cakes, twists and knots and rolls. She took the teetering stack of cake pans from the pantry and set them on every available space on the counter. Then she carefully poured a little caramel syrup into each pan.

Caramel rolls, soft and chewy and brown.

Layer cakes, white cake with white frosting and coconut on top, yellow cake with chocolate frosting, Italian cream cake, red velvet cake with cream cheese frosting, and German chocolate cake.

Children at her elbow, children at her table, dirty dishes everywhere, friends on every corner. You stop in to buy a bottle of Shephardson's vanilla—Lottie sold vanilla and cinnamon to the neighbors—and you surprise her there at the sink.

"My land!" Lottie says. "Come in!"

One of Lottie's friends, Miz Eloise, gardened and cooked with Lottie. She rode with Lottie on milk deliveries, when Lottie went around and sold her extra milk.

Miz Eloise remembered a time when she was young, when she wanted to draw close to God. Her minister told her she would need to learn to pray before she could be saved. She went to an old deacon, and he told her to get down on her knees. So Miz Eloise went out next to the old chimney and told the Lord about the cry in her heart and the sins in her life. A song came to her.

He brought me over, he carried me through.
He brought me over, he carried me through.

Nobody but you, Lord; nobody but you
could bring me over or carry me through.

Miz Eloise went to church with Lottie. One day she made a
new commitment to the Lord and decided to be baptized. Once
again the old song came to her:

He brought me over, he carried me through.
Nobody but you, Lord: nobody but you . . .

Lottie found many more Southern friends to talk with and
bake for. Many a time she baked a cake and set it carefully on a
cardboard square covered with a brand-new tinfoil square. She
delivered the cakes to her customers and friends, doctors and
dentists and family and neighbors, ladies in snazzy snakeskin
shoes and feathered hats, ladies in perfect pink dresses who
opened the door and said, "My, my! Bless you, honey."

The children grew up and the grandchildren came, one
after another, thirty-six of them. They loved to stand at Lottie's
elbow and watch her roll out the yeast dough, or trim a cake
all nice and flat, or pull a tin of cookies from the freezer. They
went to the cupboard (it smelled good, like crayons) and chose
crayons and a coloring book to color in while the rolls baked.
They stood quietly by the table where the Bible was, the thick
family Bible with all the important family dates written into
it. Sometimes they reached out and touched the thick orange
doily underneath it.

Lottie baked for them all. She wanted them all to be happy
and good. She planned her life—and all their lives—around food.
She was quick with her hugs (she smelled like cinnamon rolls
and lavender and Tic Tacs), quick with her tears and her prayers.

She sat them all down at her table and heard all the latest news. She served them all coffee and cookies. They dashed in, those children, and ate and watched and grew.

Nobody but you, my Lord, nobody but you.

If you ask the children and the grandchildren which recipe reminds them most of Grandma Lottie, they really cannot tell you. There are so many Grandma Lottie recipes and each person has adjusted the recipes and made them their own. They smile and tell you about the Jell-O surprise, with pineapple, cheese, and pecans. They talk wistfully about New Year's soup, smoky links with dill, parsley, green onions, sour dock (greens that grow wild), and potatoes, topped off with buttermilk. But finally they tell you about the leftover turkey casserole, and you think, Yes, this is the Pie Lady for me.

Because many a Pie Lady can make a Thanksgiving turkey. But the one who makes a casserole with the leftovers, and makes it grand enough that the family still thinks of it decades later? Now that's a recipe worth remembering.

You picture yourself at Lottie's table in the old gray house, or in the new red brick one the grandchildren remember. You see Lottie watching you help yourself to some of that casserole that doubles as a leftover turkey solution. You wonder which cake she made today—maybe coconut, oh yes.

You start to tell Lottie some news, and she leans close to you. You think of Tic Tacs and you smile, and you hardly know why.

"It's—it's just the best here," you say, and Lottie hugs you, and laughs.

"Well, my land," Lottie says. "My land!"

You brought me over, you carried me through.

TURKEY ALMOND CASSEROLE

4 cups chopped cooked turkey

½ cup finely chopped celery

¼ cup chopped onion

2 hard-cooked eggs, chopped

½ cup slivered toasted almonds

2 (10¾-ounce) cans cream of chicken soup

½ cup broth

¼ cup lemon juice

½ teaspoon salt

¼ teaspoon pepper

In a large bowl, mix together all ingredients. Pour into a 9 x 13-inch pan. Top with one of these three options from Lottie's similar casserole recipes: 1 cup crushed Ritz crackers mixed with ⅓ cup melted butter; 1 package herb dressing mixed with some broth and margarine (add more liquid if needed while baking); or 1 package crushed ramen noodles.

Bake for 40 minutes at 350°F.

5

The Sparkle

MIM

—and Clara and Regina and Ruthy and Amanda
and Betsy and the aunties and the in-laws
(and you, of course, and me)

Thanks be unto God for his unspeakable gift.

—2 CORINTHIANS 9:15

MIM GREW UP in Georgia, near Clark's Mill Pond. It was a friendly place, with neighbors all around ready to stop and say hey, the creeks running and talking, the trees hugging Mim with shade, her dog Pretzel ready for any exploration, her cousins ready to meet her down Shady Lane or along the creek.

Mim loved the road to Grandma Lottie's, down hills and around the curves, past the ponds with their lily pads and cypress knees, and past the woods. Grandma Lottie's was a good place to pop into, what with the house set up against the dairy farm and the cornfields, the huge trees waving welcome, the cannas tall and red in the sun. It was good to hug Grandma in all her stout stiffness. It was good to sit at her table and catch a twinkle in her eye, to learn how to serve, to watch each guest and learn their likes and not-so-likes.

Out in the woods was a clearing in the pines, which had the very best blackberry bushes. Mim loved to gather a basket of those berries and take them to her mom.

"Where did you find such big berries, almost like tame ones?" her mom would say, as she took them in her hands and looked them in the face.

Mim's mom, Frances, found acquaintances everywhere, things to learn and know and understand. She had stacks of books to study on her table and by her chair; she looked out her Georgia window and saw the wide world. Mim looked out, and dreamed, and grew. And many Sunday afternoons, she and her cousins biked the hilly miles to visit Grandma Lottie.

When Mim grew up, she married and moved to Saskatchewan. Thorns poke out of the bushes in the Canadian bush. The cold bumps into you and shivers through you. The trees stand in stately stillness, starkly aloof. Mim stood at her little kitchen window and gazed at the sky. She put the coffee on for the neighbors. She set a stack of books by her table and another by her bed. And she whipped out Grandma Lottie's recipe for caramel dumplings.

"I'm sending you this recipe from Grandma Lottie, especially for you," Mim wrote to me. "I make these often for a quick dessert. I add chopped apples for extra yumminess. Grandma sometimes added raisins."

I made caramel dumplings for lunch the very day I got the recipe from Mim. I made them in my cast iron skillet and left the lid on for the whole fifteen minutes, without peeking. When the timer rang, I saw that along one edge the dumplings still looked slightly doughy, so I turned the pan and set the timer for five minutes more.

It was so much fun to serve those rich, caramelly, old-fashioned dumplings "over ice cream." We put scoops of vanilla ice cream in our bowls and spooned the dumplings over it. I loved them so much I would have liked to make more that evening. I think you could make them in a Dutch oven over a fire, or for a special dessert when you get company some evening.

And meanwhile, Mim is learning to know the Saskatchewan trees. She can look out past the pussy willow and see the world. And Mim is only one. Grandma Lottie had thirty-six grandchildren, and many other friends who claimed her too. Each of them will smile at the memory of that sparkly lady. Mim's mom is only one. Most every mom you meet—most every teacher, every aunt—leaves a sparkle of something in lives all around her.

Regina will tell you about Winter's Best Gingersnaps, a recipe Lottie found in a magazine. Lottie kept the cookies in rusty coffee cans in her freezer, ready for grandchildren who ran in hungry after a game of Bear-around-the-Corner. Regina still makes those cookies in her new home in northern Alberta. The sugar sparkles on the rich brown cookies, the perfect thing to serve with coffee on a frosty day.

Ruthy will tell you how she copied down a roll recipe so she could bake for Lottie's grandson in her house in Georgia, how she doubles the recipe when she's cooking for a crowd, just how she kneads the dough, just how long she lets the cut rolls rise.

Clara does her housework in her home in Kentucky, dreaming about those childhood days, of slipping past the mimosa tree and into that kitchen where Grandma Lottie was in the middle of making pecan twists. She rolls her dough out now, the rich yeasty smell filling the kitchen, and tries to twist a roll just exactly the way she remembers.

Amanda will tell you how one special day she walked across the road to Grandma's house and went out into the quiet hayfield to pray. That is the place she became God's child, and it is a precious memory to her today.

Frances will remember the wonderful rolls she received—"These just didn't turn out quite right," Lottie would say—and she'll also remember the talks they had and the dishes they did together.

And the aunties will discuss roll dough recipes or the proper way to make a peanut cookie. No, no, not this way. Of course, you do it that way. (But yes, my dears, we love it every way.)

And even I am here in Kansas, making caramel dumplings!

The sparkles are there for the taking if you look for them. You can stop and have coffee with a friend and fill the hour with lovely talk about inconsequential things. You can find those moments washing dishes with your neighbor (sometimes even suds are sort of glittery) or eating cake with the dearest grandma in the world. Maybe that grandma is the only person you can imagine calling the Pie Lady—the woman who was a light for you when you were looking for God.

"She was Wendell's grandma too," said Betsy. "I still miss her dreadfully."

We can sparkle too—yes, you. And me.

CARAMEL DUMPLINGS

from Mim

Sauce

1 ¼ cup brown sugar
1 ½ cup water
1 ½ tablespoon butter

Dumplings

2 tablespoons butter
¼ cup granulated sugar
¼ teaspoon salt
1 ½ teaspoon baking powder
¾ cup flour
¼ cup milk

Bring sauce ingredients to boil in saucepan with lots of room. Simmer while you make the dumplings. For dumplings, cream together butter, sugar, and salt. Add remaining ingredients until a stiff dough forms. Drop by teaspoon into simmering sauce. Cover with lid and let steam and simmer for 15 minutes while you eat supper. Do not lift lid. Serve over ice cream.

WINTER'S BEST GINGERSNAPS

from Regina

2 cups flour
1 teaspoon ground ginger
1 teaspoon ground cloves
1 teaspoon ground cinnamon
1 teaspoon baking soda
½ teaspoon salt
¾ cup shortening
1 cup granulated sugar, plus additional for rolling
1 egg
¼ cup molasses

Heat oven to 350°F. Measure flour, ginger, cloves, cinnamon, baking soda, and salt into a bowl.

Cream shortening until soft, gradually adding 1 cup sugar. Beat until mixture is fluffy. Beat in egg and molasses, then add flour mixture and blend well. Refrigerate dough.

When dough is chilled, form 1 teaspoon dough into a ball and roll in granulated sugar. Place on ungreased baking sheets. Bake for 12–15 minutes, or until tops are slightly rounded, cracked, and lightly browned. Cool and store in airtight container.

GRANDMA'S CINNAMON ROLLS

from Ruthy

Rolls

    2 cups milk
    1 cup butter, softened
    1 cup granulated sugar'
    2 teaspoons salt
    2½ tablespoons instant potato flakes
    2 eggs
    1½ tablespoon yeast
    Enough flour to make a soft dough (6-8 cups)

Syrup

    ½ cup butter
    1½ cup brown sugar
    2 tablespoons corn syrup
    4 tablespoons water
    ½ teaspoon vanilla extract
    ½ teaspoon maple flavoring
    2 cups pecan pieces

Filling

    6 tablespoons butter, softened
    ½ cup granulated sugar
    2 tablespoons ground cinnamon

Make rolls: heat milk in microwaveable bowl until hot but not boiling, about four minutes. Meanwhile, cream together butter, sugar, and salt. Add hot milk and potato flakes. Cool to lukewarm. Add eggs. Stir yeast into one cup flour. Add to milk mixture. With mixer on low speed, add 5 more cups flour, a little at a time. Sprinkle remaining two cups flour over your counter and turn dough onto the flour. Knead until smooth, about five minutes. (You don't have to use up all the flour. You want the dough soft but not sticky. When Lottie's dough turned out sticky, she didn't like rolling it out. "Tsk tsk tsk," she murmured.) Let dough rise until doubled, at least an hour—maybe an hour and a half.

While dough is rising, make the syrup: Mix the syrup ingredients together in a saucepan and barely bring to a simmer. Pour syrup into three round (9-inch) cake pans, the deepest ones you have, or two 13 x 9-inch pans. Sprinkle with pecans.

When the dough has doubled in size, punch down, then roll out (about 8 x 24 inches) and smear with butter. Mix together granulated sugar and cinnamon and sprinkle over dough. Roll up and slice into slices about as tall as the second knuckle on your index finger. Place the rolls on top of syrup and pecans in each pan. Let rise until doubled, about 30 minutes. Bake at 375°F until a nice brown, 15-20 minutes. You have to bake these in deep pans, because the sauce bubbles as it bakes, and it will boil over short edges. But oh they are perfectly rich and delicious and I like them light, I like them dark, I like them big, I like them small.

6

Just Food

FRANCES

In all labour there is profit.

—PROVERBS 14:23

WE HAVE TO REMEMBER that all these pages are written, and all the hours are spent, and it is just food.

We know that we can spend a day reading or writing or shopping or hiking and still have a glowing moment. We know our children and grandchildren will probably choose a story over a layer cake, or a clean pair of socks over the latest recipe for blueberry buckle.

Frances learned these things from her mother Johanna. Johanna grew up helping her dad in the field, wearing a hat instead of a sunbonnet, so she didn't have to twist as far when she was driving tractor in front of the combine. In those Depression years Johanna's family often had other family staying with them. The house was full and there was much to do.

When Johanna's mother needed lunch made quickly, she called Johanna, and Johanna conquered lunch preparation in thirty minutes flat. Later, when Johanna had to go to work to help pay for a family funeral, the whipping-out-a-lunch skill was just what she needed.

Frances learned to cook with her mom, whip it out, serve it, and on to the real things.

Then Frances got married. Her mother-in-law was a true Pie Lady, and a Roll Lady, and every other kind of cooking lady. She baked to sell, rising at three. She filled her kitchen with layers of every type of delightful baked thing you can imagine. She went from one amazing meal and its attendant dishes to planning for the next. You watched and you listened and you learned.

The granddaughters learned so well that they made a cookbook filled with recipes and memories: suet pudding, mincemeat pie made with meat and raisins, turkey crunch for after-Thanksgiving turkey, favorite cookies, pecan rolls, coconut cream pie. It was a treasure.

But still. It was only food.

Food, that is, and dishes.

Frances taught children. She mowed. She did secretary work for her family. She cared for people, small people, people growing old. And in between she tried to hurry up and cook a little food.

Once she decided to tackle one more pie, after an experienced cook told her how she hurried up pies in the microwave. You mix up the fruit filling, pop it in the crust, microwave it until it's hot, and slip it in the oven.

Frances did it—mix it, pop it, mic it—each step. The filling boiled out of the pie and over. She cleaned up the mess and started the microwave once again, and the filling boiled, over and over. This time Frances dumped the whole thing and started over, examining details as she went. And there was the trouble: she had used baking powder instead of cornstarch!

Another day her mom was visiting and Frances was making one of the meals she remembered from home: potato pancakes, using leftover potatoes, for convenience and speed. The pancakes were sweet, much sweeter than anyone remembered. For once, ketchup didn't match the pancakes at all. Oh well.

After the pancake lunch, Frances went to the fridge to get out the cookie dough. You could always count on fresh hot cookies! Oh! There were the mashed potatoes that should have gone into the pancakes. The cookie dough was gone. It had obviously landed in the pancakes.

But of course those were only moments. Not every race ends in a crash. Frances learned many meals that anyone can depend on if you want to spend the morning mowing (and waving back at the grandchildren when you see them go by!) and then come in and whip out a lunch that makes the family say yum. Some races do end in a win!

One of the best things about these recipes is that after you cook them, there will be plenty of time to read a story to the little person near you. Which is great, of course. Because after all, even though it's good, it's only food.

You can make the quick version of many common recipes. I recently tried a quick and easy version of a creamy chicken casserole. The "long version" of the casserole calls for cooked rice in the bottom of a casserole dish, cooked chicken over the rice, a cheesy sour-creamy white sauce over the chicken, and buttered cornflakes over all. I put the rice on to cook and started some white sauce. Then I diced up some roasted chicken I got free from the discount grocery store (I had shopped at the end of the day) and added the chicken to the white sauce. For a special touch, I dumped some crispy rice cereal on a baking sheet with a couple of tablespoons of butter, tossed them together, and stuck the mixture in the oven to brown while the chicken-and-white sauce heated through. It was fun to serve the steaming dishes of rice, saucy chicken, and buttery crispy rice to top the lazy casserole.

Thank you, Frances—it was Pie Lady, on the run.

It's life that's grand.

LAZY CABBAGE ROLLS

Fry ground beef or sausage with diced onion. Thicken with flour or cornstarch; the amount depends on total liquids estimated. Stir in diced tomatoes and shredded cabbage. Add enough vinegar to season and add salt and pepper as desired.

Simmer until done and serve over rice. You can serve with additional vinegar and can add sour cream.

Note: To make the "long" version of cabbage rolls, break your cabbage leaves off whole, steam them (the microwave works well for this), and wrap the soft leaves around your meat mixture. Then submerge the cabbage rolls in the tomato sauce or cream sauce or whatever sauce you make and bake them in it. Lovely presentation, but more time-consuming to prepare! This is a traditional food called *gulopsi* or *halupki*. Frances's Aunt Elida, who cooked more richly than Frances's mom, put the rolls in cream sauce.

7

Phondest Pheelings and Mindful Living

RACHEL

And let the beauty of the Lord our God be upon us:
and establish thou the work of our hands upon us.

—PSALM 90:17

RACHEL'S MOM, MATILDA, was a recipe reader. She read recipes in magazines and newspapers and cut them out. She would walk to the kitchen after her nap with a paper in her hand.

"I guess I'll do this until the day I die," she said. "Cut out recipes and think I'll make them sometime."

"That's better than saying you'll die before you make it," Rachel said.

One day Rachel read a recipe in the *Edmonton Journal.* Matilda style, she cut it out and carried it to the kitchen. Several days later, she noticed the paper had included a correction of the ingredients. She marked it down, then got out her sugar and flour and set to work. The hot cross biscuits turned out dense and thick, so she did what her mother did: she studied the recipe and worked out the kinks. She was rewarded with perfect biscuits, just in time for Easter.

If you are planning to try them, start with a trip to the grocery store, because even if you have buttermilk in your fridge, it is highly unlikely that you have dried cranberries *and* dates *and* raisins *and* a jar of maraschino cherries in your cupboard. You don't want to substitute anything—you want it all.

Next, start hours ahead. The recipe tells you to refrigerate the dough, at least overnight. You can read lots of amazing bread books if you want to, books that teach you about the benefits of slow-rise bread. Or you can just trust Rachel and refrigerate these biscuits at least overnight or up to three days ahead.

When Rachel lived at home in the big old farmhouse, she and her mom baked bread to sell at farmers' markets. One of the recipes they made is cinnamon braid. Rachel and her mom would stand at the counter (surrounded by stacks of dishes from the baking). Matilda spread the cinnamon sugar on the counter. She shaped the bread into strips, rolled each strip in the cinnamon sugar, and passed the rolls to Rachel. Rachel took the sugary strands and braided them, tucked the ends under, and placed each braid in a bread pan. As Rachel finished one loaf, Matilda handed her another set of strips to braid. They made sixteen loaves working side by side, without talking. It turned out perfectly, of course. Matilda knew a thing or two.

Fridays were cinnamon roll days. Cinnamon rolls didn't get frozen, so they were made the day before market. The table was stretched out and filled with cinnamon rolls—here and there and everywhere. The day was long, and at the end of it, Rachel's dad said, "Matilda, your apron is very dirty."

Matilda looked down and agreed. "My garments are stained with cinn." Cinn-amon, that is.

When Matilda was away from her family, she sent them notes, like the one she sent to the grandchildren while they were in Phoenix:

> Phoenix doesn't pheel as phrosty in Phebruary as our pharm close to Pherintosh. It's phor that reason that your grandphather and I are pharing so phabulously here. Hope this phinds you in phine phettle. Phondest pheelings phrom Grandma & Grandpa.

Once she left a note when she stopped in and Rachel was not home:

> We did walk all the way from our place to your place. Then we did unlock your door and walked in because the butler did not take us in. Then your father did check the garage and he did see that your car was not in its designated stall. Then he did walk home to get our van and I stayed here and I did relax. I hope our presence in your home does not stress you out. We have not incurred any damages or snooped a lot.

You picture Matilda in Rachel's chair, her pen scratching away. "Where are you anyways?" she ends the note. "Shlope scheine, Mom." *Shlope scheine* means "sleep sweetly" in Low German, a perfect mom-to-daughter wish.

Today Rachel lives in an apartment on a quiet street. She still bakes to sell, but she washes dishes as she goes, keeping her counters clean. But she stands and separates lumps of bread, her hands so like Matilda's: the same short fingers, the same round fingernails, the same movements, the same results. Her hands move out and over, rolling, twisting, braiding, cutting. French bread. Cinnamon braid. Biscuits. Cookies. Croissants. She stretches out her table and fills it up.

Like Matilda, Rachel knows a thing or two. When you ask what to serve your guests one cool, end-of-summer evening, she has an idea.

"Serve them custard," Rachel says, "with baking powder biscuits, fruit, and whipped cream."

Suddenly you feel that there is nothing in the world that you want so much as custard, nothing more comforting than sitting on your couch with a cup of steaming custard in your hand.

"I wish I knew how to make custard," you say.

Rachel gives you the recipe. She tells you she prefers to take the chalazae out of the egg, and when you are alone, you google that weird word. You find out that it's the two little white things in the egg. They anchor the yolk to the shell, and if you take them out (use the eggshell to scoop them out) your custard will be perfectly smooth, without a single slimy little glob. Thank you, Rachel; we'll have custard again and again.

Like Matilda, Rachel sometimes writes notes to her friends.

This business you read these days about living mindfully . . . I've lost my piece of toast. It was tasting so good with peaches and blueberries mixed with yogurt. Where did it go? I retraced my footsteps to the bedroom where I went to get my Kobo reader. To the living room where I went to get my Bible and to see what the roaring on the street was. It was a moving van. I'm going to find my toast in some odd place. I did not eat it mindfully in its buttery crisp-ness. I'll try to do better tomorrow and keep track of my toast, because I'm not making another one now. If I'm so spinny that I eat my toast unconsciously, I don't deserve another piece. That's all I have to say about toast and living mindfully.

Baking, serving, remembering. You smell the bread bak-ing, and somehow you feel comfort and security. You savor the moment, gentle voices over coffee, the taste of a croissant with almond icing, a plate of hot biscuits, or the comfortable words "We saved a chair for you."

A word well spoken, time well spent. When life is well lived, when work is necessary but not a worry, you find the gold and silver of ordinary days. It's a Pie Lady thing to take a word and make it something to remember. It's a Pie Lady feeling to end the day tired clear to your bones, with your creations safely packaged and tucked away. The custard is per-fect. The guests may stand in the kitchen and eat right from the bowl after the meal.

"These biscuits are keepers," the children say. "Make them again."

Shlope scheine.

HOT CROSS BISCUITS

This recipe comes from the Edmonton Journal. *It's a cross between a bun and a biscuit and can be made up to three days in advance.*

2 tablespoons active dry yeast
¼ cup warm water
2 tablespoons granulated sugar, divided
2½ cups flour
1 teaspoon salt
¼ teaspoon ground cinnamon
¼ teaspoon ground nutmeg
2 teaspoons baking powder
½ teaspoon baking soda
¾ cup cold butter
¼ cup chopped dried cranberries
¼ cup chopped dates
¼ cup chopped raisins
¼ cup chopped maraschino cherries
1 cup buttermilk

Dissolve yeast in water with 1 tablespoon sugar. Separately, mix together dry ingredients, including second tablespoon sugar. Cut butter into dry ingredients until the mixture forms clumps the size of small peas, then stir in fruit.

Stir yeast mixture into buttermilk, then stir yeast-and-buttermilk mixture into flour mixture until a sticky dough forms. Cover and refrigerate until ready to bake, at least overnight. Don't bother putting a lid on tight—it will blow off.

Take the dough out of fridge 1–2 hours before you bake it.

Dust the counter with flour. Knead dough lightly in flour about six times.

Roll into rectangle about ½-inch thick. Fold into thirds, bringing short sides into middle. Roll again lightly. Pat into rectangle about ½-inch thick. Cut into squares, about 2 inches square. You'll learn what size you want. Cut a deep cross into the top of each biscuit.

Put on pans and let rise until biscuit is slightly puffy. While biscuits are rising, preheat oven to 400°F. Bake 10–12 minutes.

While still warm but not hot, pipe white icing into the cross. Adding almond extract to the icing adds one more flavor to an already flavorful morsel.

Oh, and you have to have Rachel's custard recipe.

CUSTARD

½ cup granulated sugar
2 tablespoons cornstarch
1 egg, chalazae removed
2 cups milk
Dash salt
Dash vanilla extract

Whisk together sugar, cornstarch, and egg in saucepan until smooth. Add milk and cook slowly until it boils. Remove from heat and add salt and vanilla.

8

A Gift for a Giver

SHYLA

But one thing is needful:
and Mary hath chosen that good part.

—LUKE 10:42

WHEN SHYLA HEARD the news that her Grandma Siemens
had gone to heaven, she went to her kitchen, set out her grandma's solid wooden rolling pin, and started making Grandma's
wedding cookies.

Shyla could hardly believe Grandma Siemens was gone. She
could not picture Grandma in a coffin with smooth satin sheets,
with everything nice and smooth and all expensive-looking.
Grandma loved home things, comfortable, everyday things.
If she could do the perfect thing that would say "Grandma
Siemens," Shyla thought, it would be something homemade,
preferably handwork. Grandma knew all about handwork.
She taught Shyla's mom and then Shyla to do it properly. If

only there were time to sit and sew, embroider a pillow or something.

But there were only a few hours before it was time to leave for the funeral, no time to sew. But Shyla still wanted to do something, make something. Maybe she could make a batch of wedding cookies. Shyla mixed and chilled and rolled and cut and baked, pan after wonderful pan. Her husband, Jason, started packing things, silent with understanding.

And after all, it was a good way to remember Grandma Siemens, Grandma who made something with whatever she had, with the groceries Grandpa brought home, with the things she had on hand. You might look at it and wonder, you might hope like everything that the pan would make it around the table to you. You might try something you never had seen before, or you might get the chance of a cool, soft cookie straight out of the freezer.

The cookies were for Grandma, who took your face in her hands and kissed your forehead; Grandma who baked thin-sliced potatoes on huge blackened baking sheets until they tasted like chips; Grandma who made corn fritters, who made flat crispy *rollkuchen* cookies to serve with watermelon. They were for Grandma who served mint tea made with dried mint from her garden, or who—sometimes, if you had a cough, or maybe just if it was a special day—let you drop a peppermint in your hot tea.

The solid rolling pin whirred. Shyla's fingers flew. And soon three Tupperware containers were filled with cookies for Shyla's aunties, Grandma's daughters, who would understand perfectly why she just had to make Grandma Siemens's wedding cookies. Then Shyla could pack her things up. She was ready to go, to remember.

Shyla remembered the year Grandma Siemens gave her and two of her cousins special cornhusk dolls. Grandma grew up poor, and all those years later, a cornhusk doll still seemed like a treasure to her. So the three granddaughters got the gift of a doll. Shyla loved that doll, though she wasn't a doll person. She loved the noisy, lively Siemens Christmases, the feeling of family all around, and the glory of the unexpected. She thought of the living room at Grandpa's house, the Bible verses on the walls, the dear old chairs.

Shyla packed up little-boy clothes and shoes for her boys and set them by the door. She knew it was time to go.

When Shyla saw Grandma, she saw with relief that Grandma didn't have to rest in smooth satin sheets; the aunties had lined the coffin with a well-used tapestry throw, her head on an old pillow from home. It was perfectly dear in such a homey, imperfect way. Shyla laughed and cried and remembered. She kept the cookies in the back of her van, waiting for the perfect moment.

Finally, after the graveside service, she had her chance. There in the cemetery Shyla handed anyone and everyone a wedding cookie. The cookies were a gift for Grandma, a gift from Grandma, Grandma's cookies handed out by Shyla's hands.

If you make Grandma Siemens's wedding cookies, Shyla suggests a white chocolate frosting. This recipe is from her, with special instructions. They are the perfect cookies to bake if you want a gorgeous Pie Lady moment.

I tried these cookies around Christmastime, and really, it wasn't as hard to manage the soft chocolatey dough as I expected. I rolled and baked and frosted and sprinkled and set the finished cookies on several of my largest, prettiest plates.

I looked at those cookies, and thought a little, and went and talked to my husband, Matt. "Could we have a Christmas party tonight?" I said. I called my sister-in-law and invited her family to a party.

A party, yes, or a wedding reception, a happy birthday or a silver anniversary. These cookies will fit, perfectly.

Count the things that count.

GRANDMA SIEMENS'S WEDDING COOKIES

2 eggs
2 cups granulated sugar
2 cups lard (good-quality baking lard)
2 cups buttermilk
2 teaspoons vanilla extract
1 teaspoon baking powder
3 teaspoons baking soda
1 teaspoon salt
1 cup cocoa powder
5 cups flour
Shredded coconut, for topping

Mix all ingredients—except coconut—as for cake. Refrigerate several hours. Take out a small portion of the chilled dough and return the rest to the fridge. It will be like rolling out brownie batter, but resist the urge to add more flour to the dough. Spread a fairly thick layer of flour on the counter, then sprinkle more on the dough mound so the rolling pin doesn't stick to it. Grandma's cookies often had a light dusting of flour all over them. Stop rolling at slightly over ¼-inch thick. You don't want them too thin, or it will be too frustrating to transfer them to pans. Plus, you have to roll out more if you do it too thin, and you'll get way too many cookies. Remember, you have to ice them all yet! Use cookie cutters to cut into shapes. Do not even dream of doing fancy shapes: round only, or a five-pointed star. They puff up too much to do other shapes.

Bake at 350°F for 8-10 minutes, watching very closely. Do not overbake, or they will be dry. (They do get dry if you bake them a little long—and dry cookies is not what you have in mind, of course!) Cool. Ice cookies like Shyla's grandma did—a thin layer of white frosting, sprinkled with coconut. Or try chocolate frosting sprinkled with toasted coconut—or whatever you wish. Once when it was close to Christmas, Shyla used both coconut and red-and-white peppermint Andes baking pieces for some of the cookies and left some plain, for the coconut haters. Sometimes, in a liberal moment, Grandma Siemens sprinkled them with a few chocolate chips.

9

Businesslike

TANYA

She considereth a field, and buyeth it.

—PROVERBS 31:16

TANYA LEARNED TO be a businesswoman when she was very young. Business, Tanya found, is spiced with challenges, and challenges are difficulties. But face a challenge, and you find an opportunity. Tanya's first responsibility was egg gathering— the eggs in the pen first and then the ones around the yard. It was a worthwhile work; Tanya's mom used a lot of eggs. Tanya felt especially pleased when her mom made big pancakes on a special birthday morning. Tanya loved those pancakes, and they took lots of eggs. In fact, Tanya loved them so much that one day she ate six of them. That was a true accomplishment, something great enough to report to her friends at school.

Eating six pancakes is a big undertaking for anyone. It is an especially large undertaking if the pancakes are big ones or if

64

you are a small girl. But these were worth it. One at a time, Tanya picked up a thin pancake with her thumb and forefinger, placed it on her plate, and cut it exactly in half. Then she rolled up each half, tight, and poured a pile of sugar on her plate. Finally, she dipped each roll in the sugar, carefully stamping it down to get as much sugar on it as possible. She took tiny bites, so she had more chances to stamp it in sugar. It was a great payment for the egg gathering job!

Tanya's next business venture was raising calves. Her dad raised cattle with grand names like Angus, Beefmaster, Brahman, and Brangus. Tanya thought surely she could raise a calf herself, and she did. Her dad got her a dairy calf to raise, a Holstein, and although those chores were harder than egg gathering, Tanya was up and out feeding that calf every morning, no matter the weather.

And the payment was worth it. Tanya watched her calf sell at the sale barn, and this time she bought two calves. They were Holsteins again, not Brahmans or Angus, but Tanya went to work, mixing bottles and feeding.

But business ventures do include setbacks. One of the Holsteins got sick and sicker. In a few days, Tanya and her dad sat beside it as it died. The small, quiet girl and her big dad watched and waited. Tanya never forgot that calf or the quiet time with her dad. But she did have the other calf to raise and sell.

Next she raised pigs. She bought a couple of sows and had a load of piglets to sell. The opportunity was worth the challenge in that venture!

But life had other things, not business at all—sweet things to think and dream about, and one special person named Galen.

Tanya married Galen and started cooking for him. Galen loved her concoctions.

One day Tanya asked Galen if there was anything he would particularly like her to make for him, something special his mom had made at home. "Well, I would love to taste cheese pups again," he said.

Cheese pups! Tanya knew all about cats and dogs and kittens. She knew about hot dogs and pigs-in-a-blanket. But cheese pups? Oh well, sure; Tanya figured she could make them.

Tanya told Galen about the big pancakes her mom had made for birthday mornings. Galen was horrified. Roll the cakes in sugar? That would be way too unhealthy! Oh well. The big pancakes could wait. Tanya decided to make those cheese pups. This is how she did it.

Make a (small) recipe of dinner roll dough and roll it out thin. Cut it into 2 x 5-inch rectangles. Cut a stick of ham and a stick of cheese and place them on each rectangle, carefully pinching the ends of the dough closed. Let rise for 10–15 minutes. Melt a small amount of butter in a skillet and fry the cheese pups in it. You can lean them against each other as you fry each side.

Tanya loved the cheese pups as much as Galen did. When I made them here one sunny day, my boys loved them too. Matt expected to find a strip of jalapeño inside them, and that would have been good too.

But Tanya did not forget about the pancakes. One after another, five boys joined Galen and Tanya. One day when Galen was away from home, Tanya went to the kitchen. She knew just how her mom did it. She made the special batter with lots of eggs and fresh milk. Using a paper towel to quickly grease each skillet with a little shortening, she dumped a ¼ cup of batter in each sizzling skillet. Grabbing the handles, she tipped the skillets vigorously to spread the batter over the pans. When the edges started to get dry and the middle was bubbling up all over in tiny bubbles, she loosened the edges and quickly flipped the pancakes. One down and ready to eat, and now two!

Tanya's boys didn't care whether the pancakes were healthy. They just ate them. So some mornings when Galen was busy, out working early, she made them for her boys. Those days, sometimes, Tanya only got one pancake instead of her record six. Someone told Tanya that big pancakes froze well, stacked into a sack with a piece of waxed paper between each one. Tanya never found out if that was true—there were never any leftovers to try it on.

The challenges and opportunities multiplied as the boys grew; there were hours of work and talk and good times in amazing dimensions. Tanya cooked and canned and hugged, day after day. She made special birthday meals. And who knows? Maybe someday the boys will say they want to eat something special from home, like cheese pups—or big pancakes. Each recipe is worth remembering, healthy or not. Either one will give you a Pie Lady moment, with all the messy pans and skillets to prove it.

You can handle it.

BIG PANCAKES

12 eggs
4 cups milk, divided
2 cups flour
1 teaspoon salt
3 tablespoons butter, melted
2 teaspoons granulated sugar
2 teaspoons vanilla extract

Beat eggs, then add ½ cup milk and the flour. Beat well, then add the remaining 3½ cups milk, salt, butter, sugar, and vanilla.

Heat skillet and spray with nonstick spray. Using either a ¼ or ⅓ cup measure, pour batter into skillet. Working quickly, tilt pan from side to side. As the pancake dries around the edge, carefully loosen and flip onto the other side. These pancakes fry fast; they only need to be light brown. One side will have freckles, or little brown spots. Some people eat them with cottage cheese inside, drizzled with syrup, or with sausage, fruit, or whipped cream inside.

Or eat them dipped in sugar, of course, as Tanya did. A half at a time, maybe you can down six—or more.

10

Storms and Light and Pea Soup

SHIRLEY

Who passing through the valley of Baca make it a well.

—PSALM 84:6

SHIRLEY LIVED WITH her husband in a house by the sea. Shirley's home was a place of action. The work starts early there by the sea—fishing is best at five thirty in the morning. Over and over again, you hear the boats leaving and coming back again. All summer long, fishing boats called longliners came in at the three wharves in Shirley's town and unloaded their catch of the day or their catch of the week. The air rang with the bustle of the fishing business as well as neighborly shouts, with stories and laughter. The smells of the sea and the fish were always in the air.

Shirley and her husband ran two senior homes, large places full of people and stories and life. Even outside the house,

Shirley was surrounded by life: wildflowers grew thick in between the bushes, moss grew between and around the rocks, and berries hung on bushes everywhere.

Often, storms came from the sea. Then the constant wind gathered its strength. It whipped across the flowers and grasses. It whipped around and over the houses by the sea.

Several years ago, Shirley faced a mightier storm than ever before. Her husband was dying. Shirley could not picture life without her husband, her best friend. She could not imagine life without him and his stories and his laughter. She couldn't imagine life without his boil-ups simmering away out in the woods: the potatoes, carrots, parsnips, and salt pork cooking together into a perfectly seasoned Jiggs dinner, with a circle of friends and stories around the fire.

With her husband gone, Shirley had no hope and no reason to go on. She moved into an apartment next to one of the senior homes, a place with the lovely name Shirley's Haven. But there was no comfort in that haven— just one endless day after another. Shirley was glad when night came, another day with its work behind her. In all the world, Shirley saw nothing but emptiness, empty days, empty hours. Shirley missed the action that had packed her life. She slept and worked. She drank. The darkness and depression grew.

One day Shirley saw some missionaries in her town. She felt herself drawn to them. As she got to know them better, Shirley learned to recognize the voice of God. She felt God near, promising to be her light when everything looked dark.

When Shirley gave herself to God, her heart was filled with peace and love. But she needed something to fill her hours. She needed something that would quiet the alcohol craving and give her hope and happiness.

Well.

Shirley started cooking food.

It was hard at first. She could still see her husband making Sunday Jiggs, the potatoes and all the other good things bubbling away. She could still taste his stuffed squid, his fried fish. Besides, her eyes were not as good as they used to be. The world around her was getting blurry and dim. But—she could begin. Shirley pulled out her flour and her salt and set to work. She cooked and stirred and tasted and finally called the neighbors in.

Shirley loved having people around her table. She loved the smell and the feel of the food as she worked. She loved being one of the long line of people there by the sea who took carrots and potatoes and meat and made something good.

One of the things Shirley makes for her guests is pea soup and dumplings. She will tell you all about the soup, about how years ago, the people who lived where she lives faced a big recession. Times were hard, and money was scarce, but things like split peas were cheap. Besides, they had food in their gardens, especially potatoes. In fact, the local word for "garden" means "a place to grow potatoes." So people cooked peas with potatoes and carrots and made pea soup.

Shirley meets you at the door with a hug and a kiss on your cheek. She places you at the table and ladles the rich, golden soup into each bowl. The soup is very healthy, she reminds you. It is full of fiber and protein. At the moment, you had forgotten that you need to eat healthy. Your mind is full of the sea and the wind and the fragrant smell of pea soup.

A dumpling sits in all its fluffiness on the rich, gold soup. The salt meat and the carrots and turnips make one perfect Jiggs.

It's time for a story, there in the haven by the sea. You are glad for the story, and you are glad that you are far from home. It's better than a Pie Lady moment, of course it is. It's a shelter, a comfort, a light in a world of hopelessness, there where the wild-flowers blow in the wind. Shirley smiles. She hands you soup and dumplings. She has hope and life and a work to do. And you—a stranger, maybe, who has traveled far—you have a friend.

Those who give, receive.

PEA SOUP AND DUMPLINGS

Soup

    2½ cups dried yellow split peas
    2 large onions, chopped
    1 clove garlic, minced
    3 parsnips, peeled and diced
    1 medium turnip, chopped
    3 small carrots, chopped
    2 celery stalks, chopped
    Small piece of salt meat, cubed, or 1 pound bacon
    About 10 cups water
    1 bay leaf
    Salt and pepper, as desired

Put all ingredients in a large pot; bring to boil. (Just a warning: these are approximate measures.) Simmer until split peas have dissolved, which will take a few hours. (If you want to get it done faster, soak split peas overnight. Then it will take about half the time.)

Make and add dumplings at the end of the cooking time.

Dumplings

    3 cups flour

    4 teaspoons baking powder

    1 teaspoon salt

    ½ to ¾ cup water

    ¾ cup milk

    1 egg

Stir together flour, baking powder, and salt. Mix in water, milk, and egg to make stiff dough. (The egg is actually optional, but it makes the dumplings fluffier.) Drop by ice cream scoop into boiling soup. The dumplings will take maybe 5 minutes to cook through.

People made this soup because it was economical, filling, and nutritious. Traditionally, they made it for Saturday lunch. This recipe serves around 10.

11

Cookies and Kingdoms

LORI

For where your treasure is, there will your heart be also.

—LUKE 12:34

THEY LIVED ON an old pig farm, Lori and her brother and her sisters and her mom and her dad. It was a rich place for a childhood, barns and shacks and train cars to explore and claim. There were pigs in the barns for a few years while the children grew, so of course the barns were off limits. But that was hardly even an inconvenience: who needs a barn floor when there's a train car roof to play on? Lori and her brother and her sisters scrambled over the roof and used white rock to draw beds, chairs, kitchen cupboards, and porches ten feet off the ground. They climbed carefully over the steeper roofs of the barns and peered out over the countryside.

After the pigs were gone, the children were rich in play-houses. They had endless stores of supplies: flour (the fine oily dust from the machine shop floor), sugar (sand), and leaves, grass, and twigs for added flavor or decoration. They even had a bag of cement that made wonderful chalky pies.

Sometimes they took hedge trimmers and ventured into the rows of cedar trees surrounding the farm. They cut trails and camping places out in their very own hideaway there in the trees.

One day Lori stood alone in the clearing in the trees. Stillness settled deep into her heart. The sun shone down, but even the breeze had a hard time finding a way in. Lori's heart ached with the stillness and the peace. She stood still, thinking, and wondering. Was this—maybe this—surely this is sort of how heaven is. She stepped out of the trees on quiet feet.

Behind the trees was the children's very own wilderness, a field their dad had planted to grass. Occasionally he had to mow the field, but otherwise he left it free to grow into lovely wild prairie. Even after he mowed, there were tall patches left where he had spared the birds' nests—and you never knew what other animals called that grass prairie home.

They had a whole kingdom, Lori and the rest: houses, barns, campgrounds, and wilderness. The sky was blue, the air rich and pure, heaven above them and the world at their feet. It was grand, running out in their kingdom all morning long, grander still to run in at noon, full of hunger and sun, and sit down to the lunch Mom had ready. Of course these riches came with responsibilities, dishes to do, floors to sweep and vacuum. But their heads and hearts were filled with songs and schemes, and the future stretched out, one grand, unbroken possibility.

Fall mornings came around eventually. Well-scrubbed and combed and ready for school, the children had to leave houses and barns and wait at the window until the bus pulled into the yard. The school was just down the road a few miles, a bright school with a friendly name.

Sunflower School.

Into the bus, into the school, into the group of friends. Down the hall and into the lunchroom marched a line of girls, each with her clean cotton dress, her two braids stiff and slightly damp from the morning hair combing. Lori stood with the other girls and peeked at the board where the day's menu was written out, carefully scanning the list to see what she would face in the lunchroom at noon: barbecued wieners, canned peaches, canned pears.

As the years went on, the cooks added new things to their menu: they took a whole afternoon and filled the counters with burritos. They made cheesy enchiladas, strawberry fluff, and potato boats. You'd demurely eat only half a potato boat and then go home and ask your mom to make you another one, with bologna, mashed potatoes, and melted cheese. Ranch burgers, cartons of milk. Chili, chicken noodle soup, cinnamon rolls.

Lori and the rest learned the language of lunch: if you really liked the food served, you said "Yes, please" when the cooks filled your plate. If you could hardly bear to eat something, you said "No, thanks"—and then the cooks would give you just a dab. That menu and the eating of it was a big deal. The lunch hour was life at school; it was food and riches. The children were steeped in the wealth of care around them.

Each meal was finished with dessert: huge pans of brownies, cold Jell-O cake, or a special cookie small Lori thought was way too crunchy.

Lori grew up and went to teach in other schools. She married Aaron and moved far away. Lori and Aaron moved into a house, a small white house next to a pasture with a barbed wire fence. One by one, three boys joined Aaron and Lori, filling their house and their life with noise and joy.

Sometimes at the end of a long day, they would walk out down the lane, right into the sunset. "Oh look," Rylan, the oldest, would say. "Look at the sky!" Then he would run for home, laughing and pulling at Lori's hand.

Rylan was only eight when Jesus took him home to heaven. Then how sorrow filled the little house. How they wished for all his hugs and his noise and his laughter! In those long and lonely days, Lori felt a tug from heaven, Rylan's hand on her heart, pulling her close to God. Day after day flowed by, long days, but counting up too fast. Joys came right with sorrow. Lori's mother went to heaven, and a daughter was born. And the days go by, and again and again her heart aches, or fills right up with song.

Outside Lori's house there is a treehouse in the mulberry tree, a patch of pines and oaks and cypress beyond the driveway and the pond, and a hope and a promise far beyond the farthest-off purple hill. There, beyond that farthest hill, somewhere there is heaven, our home. But today there is a meal to make, a little girl to rock and sing to, children to drive to school, meals to cook, a dress to sew. The boys run off barefoot to find their own wilderness, their very own kingdom under the sky. And Lori turns to the kitchen.

Lori's own aunt is the Sunflower School cook, and she keeps Lori posted on the food the children face. Sometimes Lori takes an idea and she makes it too, even though she is far away and Sunflower School is only a special memory, a line of little girls with braided hair.

Outside Lori's kitchen window, past the long drive, the sun is setting. She and Aaron and the children walk out. It is quiet and peaceful there, and nothing around them seems to matter much at all.

"Do you think God gives us sunsets to give us a peek into heaven?" Aaron asks. And the two of them picture a heavenly shore, and one darling boy running out to meet them. And Lori's heart aches, and the tug of love in her heart is strong.

And she stands and thinks and wonders, her heart too full for words.

Surely, O Lord, my cup overflows.

SADIE'S FAVORITES
(FROM SUNFLOWER SCHOOL)

1 cup butter
1 cup oil
1 cup brown sugar
1 cup granulated sugar
1 egg
1½ teaspoon vanilla extract
3½ cups flour
1 teaspoon salt
1 teaspoon baking soda
1 teaspoon cream of tartar
1 cup quick oats, whirred in a blender
1½ cup crispy rice cereal, ground
1½ cup mini chocolate chips

Heat oven to 350°F. Cream together butter, oil, brown sugar, granulated sugar, egg, and vanilla. Beat until fluffy. Add flour, salt, baking soda, cream of tartar, quick oats, crispy rice cereal, and chocolate chips. Bake for 10 minutes if you want tender, crispy, buttery morsels with your coffee. Or just eat big blobs of dough on the sly. I never bake them all at once; I bake batches all week, as this is a big recipe.

12

In Your Own Hands

ANNA

Take, I pray thee, my blessing that is brought to thee;
because God hath dealt graciously with me,
and because I have enough.

—GENESIS 33:11

ANNA'S HUSBAND DIED when he was in his sixties. Abe
was a man with ideas, a man of plans and adventures. They did
things, Abe and Anna. They knew things. It had been a great
life, a full life, and now it was over, and Anna was not old.

Anna did not sit at home alone. She moved to the house
she and Abe had planned to buy, a house along a quiet street
in a Kansas town. It was a house big enough to have the family
down, big enough that one of the upstairs bedrooms could be
her quilting room. She set up a quilt in that room and started
in, one quilt after another. Wedding ring quilts, satin one-piece
quilts, Anna did them all. She would let the granddaughters sit

beside her to learn to quilt—they just quilted without a knot in the thread so that Anna could pull it out and do it properly later. Friends lived down the street. Her married children lived out on the farm. She was alone, but she made her life a good one.

Then another change happened—Anna's married children moved away. Anna didn't sit alone and cry. She sold her tall white Kansas house with its friendly porch and moved to a trailer in Texas.

The trailer house sat in her son's yard, across the field from her daughter's place. The children and grandchildren were glad to have a grandma around. All the people at church claimed her as well. She was everyone's grandma.

When I learned to know Anna, she was old, and almost blind, but I did not know that. I knew she was my great-grandma, I knew she smiled a lot, I knew she had soft hands and soft, white, beautiful hair. She used a box sort of like a television to read, I knew; she set her book under it and the print showed up, large, on the screen. I knew that Grandma sorted blocks (by color, I think) into boxes so Great-Grandma Anna could make quilts, but I just figured that's what you did for a quilt-making lady.

Because that's what she did: even with her eyesight almost gone, she still made quilts. These were crazy quilts, where every piece is a different shape, and all fit together. Each quilt turns out different from another. She zig-zagged red thread over each slanted piece and then tied it together with red thread. When I think of Anna, I remember her quiet house, and a hall, and quilt blocks.

Anna took what life handed her. She treasured the life and even the things she had. One day when Grandma was dividing up some extra things, she handed Mom a paper of needles. It had been Anna's, and then Grandma's, and now it was Mom's. So many needles, you know! She could never use them all. I should blush, thinking of all the papers of needles I buy and lose. Something about that needle paper feels safe to me, kept close, taken care of. Even today I have things from Anna: an olive-green vase shaped like a watering can, a doll, a few dishes, and those quilts.

Anna chose her life and lived it. She smiled, and combed her soft, white, beautiful hair, and stitched quilts together. She gave a cookbook to her granddaughter, an extra cookbook, I suppose, but one with old recipes in it that the granddaughter still uses many years later. She gave vases and hugs to great-granddaughters.

She gave advice.

"Keep the floor clean," she told Grandma. "The whole house will feel clean."

She gave helpful hints. "Cakes don't like to climb up greased walls," she said. "Just grease the bottom of the pan, so the cake rises higher."

If only I can remember to give something—give anything. A vase, a hug, a piece of advice—because my life is good, God gave it to me, I have enough. "This is for you."

Anna also gave recipes. I found one of them in a cookbook put together by the ladies at the Texas church. Anna was already gone when they made the cookbook, but they included this recipe in memory of her. I made it once when we had a neighbor boy working for us, and I will never forget how like a Pie Lady I felt as he enjoyed this homey dish.

These days, I often use a mix of boneless chicken breasts and thighs. And I add a couple of teaspoons of bouillon and a clove of garlic to the chicken while I cook it. Cook the chicken a long time, until it falls apart. You can use buttered cracker crumbs instead of cornflakes, any kind of buttery cracker mixed with half a stick of melted butter. You can also skip the chicken soup—just thicken your broth, like making gravy, and add some cream.

And there's another recipe here for Russian pancakes. I couldn't leave it out, even though it is so much like Tanya's Big Pancakes. This one is thanks to Aunt Juanita, a sweet and gracious and very fun woman who married Anna's youngest son. Juanita says, "I was traveling with Emory's mother one day when she gave this to me. It's our favorite!"

When I make these Russian pancakes, we put crumbled sausage in them and roll them up, topping them with cream syrup. I even sort of like running back and forth between the table and the stove, frying as we eat. Set your burner pretty close to high and heat your skillet until it is hot. Dump the batter in the center of the skillet and tip the skillet every way so it is as thin as you can get it. Fry it as long as you can on the first side, but only until it is nicely browned. Then stick a big turner underneath it, and flip. Then you just fry the second side for a little bit and it is done. Sometimes I don't fry the first side quite long enough, and it tears, but once I get into it, and flip a pancake as big as the skillet, I feel Accomplished—for the moment, at least, and isn't that all that matters?

This is for you.

CHICKEN NOODLE CASSEROLE

1 small chicken
½ cup chopped onion
1 medium package noodles, cooked
½ cup grated cheddar cheese
2 cups crushed cornflakes
Salt and pepper, as desired

White sauce
⅓ cup butter
3 tablespoons flour
2 cups chicken broth
1 (10¾-ounce) can cream of chicken soup

Cook chicken and onion in 3 cups water until chicken is done. Remove chicken from bones and shred meat. Combine chicken and cooked noodles in buttered baking dish.

Make white sauce: Blend butter and flour in a saucepan; add broth and bring to a boil. Boil for 3 minutes. Add cream of chicken soup to white sauce and pour this over the noodle mixture. Sprinkle with grated cheese and top with cornflakes. Bake for 45 minutes at 350°F.

RUSSIAN PANCAKES

2 eggs, beaten
2 cups milk
⅓ cup vegetable oil
1 teaspoon salt
1½ cup flour

Combine eggs, milk, oil, salt, and flour. Mix well. Pour
½ cup batter onto hot griddle to make large pancakes.

13

A Little Child Shall Lead

LENORA

Whosoever shall receive this child in my name
receiveth me.

—LUKE 9:48

LENORA'S SECOND CHILD was a girl, a beautiful dark-haired baby. She was born after a long and difficult birth. Lenora and her husband, Leon, named the baby Carol.

Carol did not do things as quickly as other children. It took a long time for her to learn to crawl, and she didn't learn to walk until she was three.

"Oh, she's all right," the doctor said, when they took her in to see him. "She's just slow, and maybe hard of hearing."

The next year they tried again, back again to the doctor. "Yes," the doctor said at last, "Carol's brain was damaged at her birth."

It was devastating news. There was no cure, no help. Leon and Lenora took Carol home. They were two young people with a small family and a big problem. Up until then, they had lived life without thinking much about it. Heaven was a long way off, and hardly on their minds. Life was good, and almost easy. But this—this was bigger than anything they had ever imagined. They did not stop to think about how or why; it was too big for that.

"God sent us Carol," Leon said. The two of them got on their knees and prayed to God, and the huge block in their path became the gate of heaven.

It wasn't easy. Of course it wasn't easy. Carol never did learn very much. She'd pick up the dishtowel to help dry the dishes, though she never did dry any water off them. She'd write her name on the chalkboard, though she never mastered the r in it: c-a-o-l, she'd write.

Leon and Lenora had other children, a busy, noisy family who grew up all around Carol. Those were full days, busy days, children running in and out, making hideouts in the woods, houses in the hay bales, and dreaming up games they could play on their bikes. They soon learned how to help, in the shop and in the house. And all too soon they were off to school, waiting for the bus at the end of the drive with their square lunchboxes in their hands. They were off every morning at 7:40, and one day flew after another.

The years sped by. It was good to have a reminder of what it meant to be a child, a truly helpless child, though it was also a lot of extra work. "Carol is the only one of us with a ticket straight to heaven," Lenora reminded the rest of the children.

"God sent her," Leon added.

Leon had a lawn mower business, with a bell rope strung across the driveway. When someone drove over that rope, the bell rang in his shop and in the house: "Ding, ding!" Sometimes the ring meant a customer was bringing lawn equipment for Leon to fix. Other times it was someone stopping by for one of Lenora's pies.

Because Lenora was a Pie Lady. Often the phone rang on the wall and you heard Lenora pick it up and answer in her cheerful singsong voice, "Hello?"

Then someone on the other end asked if Miz Ensz could make some pies. Yes, why yes, she could make some pies. What kind?

So the bell would ring and the screen door would slam and Lenora would step out of the house with her plastic pie carriers (she could stack up five or six) and a big Pie Lady smile.

"Oh, they ahh *beauuutiful!*" the customer would say.

It was work Lenora loved to do, all those coconut cream pies, and lots of chocolate, lemon, and peanut butter pies too. She mixed big batches of pie filling and stirred it vigorously to keep it from scorching as it popped and bubbled on the stove. Then she added peanut butter crumbs to some of the pudding, chocolate to some, coconut to some, piled each one into a baked crust and topped them with melt-in-your-mouth meringue. After the meringue was browned in the oven, she set the pies on a cooling rack, and truly they were a picture. Lenora wiped her hands on her worn terrycloth apron, did the dishes and wiped off the countertops, and waited for the bell to ding, telling her she had a customer.

She had baked pies all her life, of course. It was only now, when they lived closer to town, that she could bake for others. And bake she did! She baked for weddings, funerals, and special occasions. She baked many pies for people who had lost loved ones, an "I care about you" gift of comfort food.

The days were full, and the weeks. Carol was grown up now and lived in a home where they knew how to care for special people like her. They knew she was happy there. But when Sunday came, the family got in the car and went and took her on a drive. Carol loved the drives, and they loved to take her, but when the drive was over, they felt that she hated the end of the drive as much as they did. She was theirs, and they were hers, after all.

And the days went on, and the months and the years, and Lenora went on baking for her children, her customers, her neighbors and friends. She put crusts in the freezer. She baked the crusts and filled them. When Leon and Lenora got so old they had to move to an assisted living center, there were seventeen pie crusts in her freezer.

Carol went to heaven before her parents did. She was only in her fifties, but her heart gave out, and she went home to God. Then how they missed those Sunday drives, the uncluttered simplicity of their special child!

"If ever we make it to heaven," Leon would say, "if ever Lenora or I, or any of our children—" He was old by then, and gentle, and you felt that yes, oh yes, he knew the way. "If ever we make it there," he would say, "it will be because of her."

And Lenora would smile, and cry, and nod her head. Carol was hers, Carol was God's, the life of her special child showed them the way.

Jesus loves me.

LENORA'S PIE

Pie crust
>   6 cups flour (White Lily brand is best)
>   2 rounded teaspoons baking powder
>   3 rounded teaspoons salt
>   3¼ cups shortening
>   1¼ cup water
>   2 eggs
>   2 tablespoons vinegar

Stir together flour, baking powder, and salt with fork. Cut in shortening. Separately, mix together water, eggs, and vinegar. Add to flour mixture. Mix just until it clings together well, then refrigerate for several hours.

Heat oven to 375°F. Roll out crust. When putting in the pie pan, leave an overhanging edge or the crust will shrink. Press onto the edge of the pan. Crimp as desired. (Lenora crimped her pies with big crimps, then tried to cover it with meringue!) Poke holes liberally with fork. Bake until light brown, 10–12 minutes. Makes 6 crusts.

Pudding
>   ¾ cup granulated sugar
>   ⅓ rounded cup cornstarch
>   ¼ teaspoon salt
>   3 egg yolks, beaten
>   2½ cups milk, scalded
>   2 tablespoons margarine
>   1 teaspoon vanilla extract

Mix together sugar, cornstarch, salt, and egg yolks. Whisk mixture into hot scalded milk, stirring constantly, until thick and bubbly. Add margarine and vanilla. Try one of the following variations. (If using meringue, bake as instructed.)

Chocolate: Add ½ cup chocolate chips to pudding. Place in baked pie shell and top with meringue (see recipe on p. 21) or whipped cream.

Coconut: Add 1 cup shredded coconut to pudding. Place in baked pie shell and top with meringue or whipped cream.

Peanut butter: Mix together 1 cup powdered sugar and ½ cup peanut butter. Put half in bottom of crust, cover with meringue or whipped cream, and spoon the remaining peanut butter mixture on top of the meringue or whipped cream.

14

Silver and Rose

VI

Honour all men.

—1 PETER 2:17

VI. SHE WAS the big sister you could depend on, the friend you call every day. In your own family, in the north country, in towns or on farms, there is one thing you can always find: friends. Old friends, new friends. Friends to talk with, laugh with, sing with. Friends to share your joys and sorrows with.

You take your laughter wherever you go, you take the peace in your heart. Vi loved to tell how light and happy she had felt when she gave her heart to God. She loved to tell what she believed, that God is near, that God is real, that God is love.

Vi married Bert and they raised a lively family of six in a house full of noise and ideas. Life was filled with adventure— new places, new faces, new work to do. The years flew by, the work and the talk and good times. Vi cooked and cleaned and listened and laughed. She worked and helped and prayed.

After the children left home, Vi kept cooking in her yellow kitchen. She stretched out the table and spread it with a silvery cloth. Then she went to the china cupboard, opened the glass doors, and took out the dishes.

Those dishes. They were a gift from Bert, chosen especially for Vi. Bert had grown up with a mother who loved her dishes and taught her boys to treat them carefully. Be careful, be careful, Bert's mother taught them—you'll face something not pleasant if you break one of my dishes! They learned, and they learned well. When he married Vi, Bert bought her dishes, lovely china dishes, white dishes with pink moss roses sprinkled across them. He bought beautiful rose glasses to match the dishes, and a china cupboard to store the dishes in.

It was a good gift for Vi, who loved people. She spread the silvery cloth, set out the pink flowered china and the rose goblets, set rose-colored cloth napkins beside each place setting, shining silverware straight in its place, and prepared a lovely meal. Then the table was filled: the cousins jostling each other and laughing, the pile of potatoes steaming, the steak rich in its gravy, the vegetable bowl heaped up, the salad full of color, the grown children and their talk filling the table and the room. And that was the best, the very best. That was the reason Vi had worked and planned. Family or friends, these were her guests.

And Vi loved guests. Oh, they were worth the hours she spent in the yellow kitchen, cooking. They were worth every minute of preparation, worth every plan. Vi would fill the goblets with ice and tea, check to make sure the table was right, check the food and do last-minute things while Bert watched the driveway. You walked in the house and got a welcome. You stepped up to the table and stood taller—you were a guest, and suddenly that felt grand.

Who wouldn't feel grand, at a silvery cloth, with rose napkins and goblets against rose-flowered plates? Who wouldn't feel grand, with baked steak on a platter and a fresh pumpkin pie just in sight? Who wouldn't feel grand and ready for a visit?

Because people are grand. All people, any people. You can talk with Miss Kansas or with your own grandchildren. You can talk with the neighbor or the waitress or anyone you meet.

"You never need to be afraid of anybody," Vi used to say. "Why, even Queen Elizabeth does the same things we do. We're all just people."

In fact, Vi shared a birthday with the queen. One year she sent the queen a birthday card and received a reply from the queen's lady-in-waiting. We're all just people, yes, special people—every one of us.

It's not a big thing, making someone feel grand. It's a certain silvery thing done by someone who lives down the street, the friend who loves to laugh with you, the neighbor who shares her morning with you, your sister, your mom, your friend.

It's a mom, of course. It's the mom who warmed pajamas by the stove in the winter, who wrapped the children up and held them on her lap. It's the mom who always believes in you, who knows that if you want to do it, you can. (Why yes, you can do it! Bake a pumpkin pie? Make a friend? Build a home? Oh definitely! You could be president, daughter dear, if that's what you wish! You can do it, whatever it is! Of course you can!)

It's a sister, maybe, the one who calls you every day. It's the grandma who stops you in the center aisle after Sunday service.

It's the friend who cares about how you feel, who listens to you and shares with you. It's the little bit of extra that makes life shine.

The dishes were Bert's, and the welcome and the prayer. But the dinner was Vi's, and the visit, and the long, silvery cloth. Life is good, you know, friends are gold, guests are blessings— and this day, this hour, it really is grand.

Stand up and shine.

SMOTHERED STEAK

Here's the recipe for Vi's steak, to be served on china plates.

Start with enough steak to feed a crowd: chuck steak or round steak is fine. Thaw the steak and pound it. (Vi liked to pound it with the edge of a plate. This takes a while, but it makes it good. Your arm will be tired, I know.) Dredge each piece in flour, salt, and pepper as desired—a couple spoonfuls of salt, I think, for each cup of flour. Fry in a little hot oil over a medium heat and transfer to a baking dish. Reserve the drippings to make a gravy, adding cream of mushroom soup and milk to right consistency—a sort of thin gravy, because it thickens as it bakes.

Pour gravy over steak and place in a 250°F oven for several hours, at least 2 hours. Serve with fluffy mashed potatoes, green beans, and lettuce salad. Finish the meal with pumpkin pie for a year-round treat. It's fit for a king; it's Pie Lady grand!

15

Seeing Balloons

ELSIE

*Give, and it shall be given unto you; good measure,
pressed down, and shaken together, and running over.*

—LUKE 6:38

I LEARNED ABOUT GIVING from a woman in my town.
I didn't know Elsie, but I had heard of her. Rather, I had read
of her. One day in our local newspaper, there was an article
about a woman who volunteered by visiting at the care home.
She wasn't just any visitor who volunteered an hour a week for
a year or two. Oh no. She visited the care home every week for
more than twenty years.

I watched the paper after that. They published the guest list
of the care home residents, and there it was, every week, on
quite a few of those lists: Elsie. Elsie. Elsie. I thought about her
a lot. What kind of a woman would visit the care home every
week for years and years? She must be a very special person.

One day my friends and I and our children took a birthday party to the care home. One of the tables of residents who attended the party was a group of women who laughed and talked like old friends. I stood and watched them and wished I could be a part of their group—they looked like they were having a really good time.

The white-haired woman in the middle of it all noticed me watching, with no one to talk to.

"Are those your children?" she asked me.

"This one is mine," I said.

"Beautiful children." The woman smiled at the children and at me.

"Thank you. How long have you lived here?"

"Oh, almost a year now—a year next month."

"Do you like it here?"

"Oh, I love it. I've been coming for many years, you know, visiting, so I have lots of friends here. We have good times."

She had visited often, she said. Maybe I had found her! I decided to risk it. "You know, I read in the newspaper once about a woman who visited here regularly," I said. "Are you—"

"Yes, I'm Elsie."

"You are! I've wanted to meet you ever since I read that newspaper story. How long did you visit here?"

"Well, I started when my mom moved in here, and I just never stopped, for twenty-nine years. Then my children decided I needed to move in myself—when my eyes got so bad, you know. I like it, though."

"It seems like I remember the paper said you'd been out picking apples."

"Could be. I did have apple trees out at the farm."

I had actually met her, and she felt like a friend! Whenever I saw Elsie after that, I asked her about her life. She answered my questions about the old days but she always came back to the present.

"Well," she'd say, "I came to this area as a high school student. My grandma lived in town here and she wasn't well, so I moved out from my hometown to help her. My, but I was shy in those days!" Then a few minutes later she'd be talking about her brother, who was in a care home several hours away and sometimes called her on his cell phone. Or she'd tell me that yes, she'd had holiday gatherings at her place—most of them, actually, because she had plenty of room for a spread-out table. Then she'd tell me about the friend she'd made down the hall, the woman she took walks with every day.

I kept going to see Elsie, trying to unlock the key to her giving, wondering when she was going to receive a heaped-up, shaken-together, running-over return.

Elsie told me about her children and about the house she helped her husband build. She told me about the pasture around the house and the farm they bought. She was pleased to have her son and daughter-in-law living in her place, and I thought it sounded wonderful: a house Elsie and her husband built with their own hands, a pasture and a creek, spring flowers and apple trees. I pictured it in my mind, and wondered, until one Sunday afternoon Matt drove me by there. The pasture was picturesque, but the house was just a normal farmhouse and I couldn't even see the apple trees. For Elsie, the ordinary was beautiful.

Slowly Elsie's health failed. One evening we went to the care home to sing to the residents, and Elsie grabbed my hand.

"I loved the songs," she said. "The messages in them were so true—the messages." Her eyes were soft, her voice sweet.

When I think of Elsie, I think of her love of today. I remember how she loved her house and her children. I think of the pasture and the trees and the family gatherings she hosted. I remember how she'd talk about her husband and say softly, "He was a good husband to me." I remember Elsie at the rest home surrounded by friends, and the new friend she made there who walked with her and had every lunch and tea by her side. Somehow I think I know what Elsie would say about her life. "It was a good life for me, a good life. I had lots of good times."

Because Elsie saw the heaped-up beauty of each day, she missed other things. She missed frustrations of busy days and found memory-making family times. She missed the emptiness of a quiet house and found people who waited to see her walk in the door. She missed the loneliness of old age and found hallways filled with friends.

I remember one icy day I stopped in and met Elsie in the hall. She was pushing her walker, with two bright balloons attached to the side. We said hello and a nurse told me it was Elsie's birthday. Elsie had no time to talk that day; she was pushing that balloon-lit walker to the bingo game.

When Elsie's family held a garage sale out at the farm, I went out to see if there was anything I could buy, any Elsie treasure. There was a trailer full of household things but hardly a treasure in sight. A few jars, a few cookbooks, and other well-used things. I found a water pitcher with lemons painted on it. I found a cookbook with Elsie's handwriting in it.

The cookbook was an old one; it was a whole book of salads, many of them gelatin salads. "Salads are always in good taste," the book says. It has pages of salad guides and calorie charts and includes hints on "serving with a flair." I turned the pages and found lots of marked recipes—some marked *good*, some *delicious*. One even had coconut prices written beside it. I saw that Elsie had cooked the way I do, with her cookbook nearby: the marked recipes and turned-down pages have spots on them from those long-ago family dinner days.

I chose one of Elsie's recipes to share with you. She marked this one "Polly's Party." Hopefully, if you try it, you have to go to the store for groceries. And if you do, maybe you can stop in at the care home and say hello to a friend, just for Elsie's sake. When I think of Elsie, I remember the twinkle in her eyes, her chuckle, and the many things she was always doing. I smile, and thank God for my good husband, the home I love, and the friends around me. And I look for bright balloons on every walker.

Friends are everywhere.

POLLY'S PARTY SALAD

  1 cup pineapple chunks
  1 cup mandarin oranges (drained if using canned)
  1 cup shredded coconut (or maybe bananas)
  1 cup mini marshmallows
  1 cup whipped cream

Mix all ingredients together and refrigerate.

16

Saturday

YVETTE

Arise; for this matter belongeth unto thee:
we also will be with thee.

—EZRA 10:4

FOR AS FAR back as Yvette can remember, something had been wrong with her grandma's oven door. It never bothered Grandma—she just took a rubber spatula and wedged it between the oven door and the frame to close the door good and tight.

Yvette used to stand back and watch Grandma wiggle that spatula into place. She watched Grandma fry meat at the stove and set the table full of dishes. It was something to watch, Grandma's stove, Grandma's table. It was something to see.

Yvette loved to hear Grandma tell stories all about the people she knew and loved. Grandma had married Grandpa in Kansas when she was still a teenager. Their wedding day was

April 7, 1935, only a week before the terrible dust storm rolled into western Kansas—the storm people talked about for years and years. It wasn't the only dust storm, either. Other storms followed it. Grandpa and Grandma were young then, farming, watching storm clouds and dirt and waiting for rain. They stuck it out for a couple of years, but finally they packed up and headed for California.

It was a long trip, and a slow one, the trip that took them far away from the dust storms. Grandma loved California, the newness of it, the beauty of it, the greenness of it. She loved the rivers and the orchards—whole fields of fruit and nut trees. But she didn't see her parents again for six whole years.

Yvette sat and listened to the stories and imagined days spent on long, narrow, dusty roads. She imagined looking for a house in a brand-new place, finding new work and new friends. It sounded exciting, really. It would be fun to do new things in your own way. Yvette was glad Grandma had gotten out of those dust storms. She was glad California was the place she called home.

Yvette liked to go to Grandma's on Saturdays. Those were the days when things really happened at Grandma's. Even when she was little, Yvette knew the Saturday plan.

Every Saturday, for as long as anyone could remember, Grandma got up early. She set her seven daughters to work. The girls mowed the yard, cleaned the house, and washed the blue Oldsmobile. Grandma set to work herself, attacking the laundry mountains. She worked through them a load at a time: darks, lights, whites, good clothes, everyday clothes, towels. The thin towels flapped dry in no time out on the clothesline. Grandma took them in and folded them into tall stacks. But many of the clothes went straight to the ironing room. Yvette used to stand at the door of that room and stare at the mountain of clothes waiting to be ironed.

You may love or you may really not love a Saturday plan. You may say, "I really can't face Sunday unless my bathrooms are clean," or you may say, "I don't like to waste my Saturdays cleaning house." You may clean without thinking about it on Saturday, or you may clean early in the week and take Saturday off. Or you may do as I did when I started keeping house: just skip it for quite a while and hope that your friends don't happen to stop in.

But there is one really great thing about a Saturday plan: you start out in the morning knowing just what you will do, and even approximately how long it will take you. You can dream out a whole story while you fold the towels, and you can call your sister while you mop the floor. If you know the minute you normally stop and thaw the hamburger for lunch, you don't have to figure anything out. You just vacuum rugs until exactly 11:20, according to plan.

When all the clothes were finally clean, Grandma took the just-washed Oldsmobile to town and bought groceries to re-stock her cupboards. Then she went home and fixed tacos for supper. Yvette loved to be at Grandma's for those Saturday tacos. She wasn't sure what it was that made them so perfect— the melted cheese, the spicy beans, or the chilled bottles of Pepsi that Grandpa carried to the table.

In her seat beside the younger aunts, Yvette cleaned her plate. Sometimes she took a second taco. And she remembered those tacos for years, the exact, perfect flavor of them. Forty years later, in the midst of normal days—good days and long days, busy-but-happy or looking-toward-heaven days—she tried hard to re-create them, right down to the chilled bottle of Pepsi.

Yvette wrote down the taco recipe. You can try them even if your Saturday doesn't include seven daughters mowing and cleaning and washing the car while you do the week's laundry and shopping. You can try them even if your Saturday is spent at a mission house by a hospital complex, where you are an observer of sorrows and a helper and friend.

Make them on any busy day, sprinkle the cheese over the hot, spicy meat, and you will have that Pie Lady feeling of something Accomplished. The cheese will melt over the perfectly spiced meat—"These are good," someone will say. Pass the Pepsi.

A good day is in the plans.

SATURDAY SUPPER TACOS

1 pound ground beef
1 onion, chopped
Salt, as desired
½ teaspoon chili powder
1 (15½-ounce) can pinto beans in chili sauce
Corn tortillas
About 1 cup vegetable oil (depending on your skillet)
Grated cheese

Fry ground beef with onion and salt. Add chili powder and approximately half a can of beans. Simmer.

Pour vegetable oil into your skillet (the oil should cover the bottom, but not be too deep) and turn heat to high. When the oil feels hot when you hold your hand a couple of inches above the skillet, fry tortillas: lay tortilla flat in the oil, pick up the edge with a tongs, and fold it in half. Then turn the tortilla with the tongs to fry the other side. Immediately take the tortilla out of the oil and turn upside down to drain on paper towels.

When all the tortillas are heated, place a little meat mixture in each one and sprinkle with cheese. Place in baking dish and heat in oven until cheese is melted. Enjoy with ice-cold bottled Pepsi.

17

My Time and Place

ESTHER

*Who knoweth whether thou art come to the kingdom
for such a time as this?*

—ESTHER 4:14

ESTHER WAS BORN in a little house on the Canadian plains, where well-tended farms grew tall under a wide blue sky. When she was still a little girl with dark thick braids, she moved with her family to California. There she lived in the land of sun, where the grapes grew sweet and ripe and water flowed down the river and through the canals to irrigate the fields. Those canals were perfect for swimming and splashing and for cooling off on a hot California day. Esther and her family found good things and good friends in California.

But something was calling them back. Esther was only nine when they left California behind. Dad and Mom and all seven children piled into the Studebaker car and headed north to the Canadian prairie. It was a big place, a wide place, this land of opportunity. It was a place for plans and ideas, a wonderful place to grow up under the sun and the sky. Here the wind called and ran across the open spaces, playing with the laughing grasses and shouting lullabies under the stars.

When she was twenty-four years old, Esther married tall, blond Alvin. They worked and planned and dreamed together, and finally followed a dream across the mountains to beautiful British Columbia. There in the farmhouse the wind was nothing but a whisper. Clouds softened the skies and dropped down the rain.

Things grew in the mountain country, and trees were rich with fruit. Esther picked and cooked and canned apples, peaches, and pears. She bought salmon from the people who lived down by the river and canned until her cellar shelves sagged with the riches. The children ran and worked and played and spent hours in the huge cherry tree up on the hill. They picked cherries and ate cherries and shot pits of cherries out of their mouths and down the hill. They worked along with Esther and helped Alvin in the dairy, where he brought in bucket after bucket of fresh milk.

The winters were mild, and spring came early. Esther's sisters lived around the corner, her four brothers down the road. Cousins ran and played, and sisters shared days. Every month or so, when the boys' hair got long, Alvin and Esther drove the family down to their brother's place. Then the jolly times rolled!

Each winter Alvin and Esther packed up the family and traveled across the mountain and back to their folks' places on the prairie. There in the chill of winter, the skies sparkled with the glory of the galaxies. The heavens rejoiced, the people praised, the stars sang their own alleluia. But best of all was the end of the road, and Grandpa's farm, and the people waiting. It was Christmastime then.

You can settle in a house by the side of the sea or you can travel to mountains and hills. But there's more than mountain grandeur that you need for a family of eight—there's something you can find in the land of opportunity, where the work is large and the days are long. The mountain country was beautiful and the days were mild, but Alvin and Esther packed up their family and headed home.

Home! And the work was much and the friends many. Esther loved to fill the table with good things and invite the neighbors in. Mashed potatoes, honey chicken, thick white gravy—you were glad to be there at Esther's table.

The days passed, the years flew, and once again Esther and Alvin moved on to mountain country. And the children grew up, and left home, and Alvin and Esther grew older. One life-changing day, Alvin and Esther's son and grandson were on their way to town to buy a new rocking chair for Mama and the new baby when they had an accident. That sad day they flew away to heaven. It was so sudden, so huge, such an emptiness, such a walk in the valley of sorrow! Day after day on those long weary days, Alvin and Esther went over to their son's home and shared hours and sorrows with the lonely mama and her two little boys.

Then Alvin spent several years fighting cancer and then he too was gone. And then another time of sorrow, when the youngest daughter had an accident and the angels came again. Those were dark days, and Esther bent under the wind. But she looked up to God and somehow kept on.

She had always kept on, meeting new people and learning new things. At forty, Esther learned to drive. She had braved hours of practice at backing up and parallel parking for the triumph of a driver's license. At eighty, Esther tucked her new cell phone in the trunk of the car and drove across the province to see her daughter. The thing in front of her, Esther did it. A license, a drive, a new phone—she could do it.

At ninety-two, Esther taught her daughter-in-law to make pierogies: perfect, flaky pierogies, a hundred at a time. She called her daughter-in-law on that planned-for morning. "Oh, I'm so excited!" Esther said. All day, she watched and advised and helped until finally they had accomplished the whole hundred. "That should be enough," Esther said—enough for supper tonight and some to freeze for another busy day. At ninety-two, she knew a thing or two. She knew how to make the most of the day she had in her hands, how to face things straight on.

Straight on, straight on, one day at a time, faithful as a pilgrim, gracious as a queen, under a wide blue sky.

There's a work for me to do; there's a place for me to be.

ESTHER'S RECIPE FOR PIEROGIES AND ONION GRAVY

Pierogies
    3 cups flour
    ⅓ cup oil
    1½–1¾ cup water
    1⅛ cups dry cottage cheese
    1 cup creamed cottage cheese
    1 egg, slightly beaten
    Salt and pepper, as desired

Mix flour, oil, and water together to make a soft dough.
Add more water or milk if needed for a softer dough.
Separately, mix together cottage cheeses, egg, salt, and
pepper. Set aside.

Roll out the dough to a thickness of about ⅜ inch. Cut out
circles of dough using your pierogi dough press (if you
have one—if not, you can use a large biscuit cutter or a
drinking glass). Then reroll the cut-out shape into a still thinner one. Gently lay the dough over the press to overlap the
edges. Place about a tablespoon of cottage cheese filling
onto one half; press together tightly to seal the top and
bottom pieces of dough. If you don't have a pierogi dough
press, roll out the dough quite thin and cut into rounds 4 or
5 inches in diameter. Place a spoonful of filling onto each
round. Fold round in half and seal edges well with your
fingers or a fork. (This version of the recipe does not make
a hundred; a dozen or so will do.)

Place pierogies on a baking sheet; transfer the pan to
the freezer to chill for at least 20 minutes. This makes the
pierogies less likely to separate during boiling. Gently drop
the chilled pierogies into boiling water; boil for 4 minutes.

Drain off water. Then fry in butter in a nonstick pan, on a moderate heat, to a golden brown. Serve with onion gravy.

You can leave the pierogies in the freezer, of course, and boil and fry them at a later date.

Onion Gravy
  ½ onion, finely chopped
  1 tablespoon butter
  ⅓ cup flour
  2 cups milk
  Sour cream

Sauté onion in butter. Add flour and mix in thoroughly. Add milk and stir until it bubbles and is thickened. Season with salt and pepper to taste. Just before serving, add 1 dollop sour cream. Do not boil after adding sour cream.

Esther's menu on Pierogie nights:
• Pierogies onion gravy to pour over pierogies

• Spaghetti topped with Roger's Golden Syrup

• Lettuce salad

• Vegetable such as corn

• Dessert

18

Beef Country and Cornmeal Dreams

CARLOTTA

He hath made everything beautiful.

—ECCLESIASTES 3:11

CARLOTTA LIVES IN a house on a farm in Nebraska. Nebraska is beef country, farm country, big open-grass country. In Nebraska you travel down wide dirt roads and past small friendly houses to small friendly towns. They grow corn to feed to the cattle, and they raise cattle for beef. They serve beef in all those friendly houses and in every small café. It is far from Wisconsin, the land of lakes, where Carlotta grew up.

Wisconsin is a land of green summer, red fall, and white winter. It's a place where you can spend your days helping your dad with his bees, bottling up the honey, and driving down curvy paved roads and past tall farmhouses, with their gardens and flowers, past big red barns and contented milk cows. It's a place where you go back into the woods to help your brother tap the trees for sap and boil it down.

Carlotta spent hours outside in her playhouse or playing with her cats. Why waste a nice day in the house? Sometimes her big brothers built tunnels and houses in the hayloft. Those were the best days of all—climbing through the tunnels, setting up house, making her own special spot in the top of the barn.

But the years flew by, and Carlotta was all grown up. She spent two years in her own spot up in another barn, a barn that had been made into a small private school. There Carlotta taught school to first and second graders. Teaching is a good work, full of questions and laughter and fingerpaint and flashcards. Teaching means running with the children at recess and reading them stories in the quiet classroom after lunch. Teaching means doing whatever it takes to get children to learn.

After teaching two years in Wisconsin, Carlotta lived in Nebraska, first as a schoolteacher and later as a bride.

The new home was perfect. It was her own spot on the earth, and it was fun to make it feel like hers. Carlotta set up her things and arranged and rearranged. She found places for all her wedding gifts and her new kitchen things. She filled her cupboards with the first sacks of groceries.

To think that it was only a few years back when Carlotta was out on the farm in Wisconsin, raising a pig for the family to butcher. She got to be such good friends with that bound-for-sausage pig. If he got out, her dad and brothers would call Carlotta, and he would just follow her into his pen.

It was just a little while ago that she was raising calves, helping her dad with the milking, raising chickens, gathering eggs, and carrying feed and water—oh, and watching out for the rooster. That biggest and most beautiful rooster! What do you do with a mean rooster, please, a rooster you know very well? You take him to the sale barn in his own small cage and sell him to the highest bidder, asking no questions about what the buyer will do with him. And then you pocket your eight dollars and enjoy your peace!

And now for Nebraska—Nebraska, that is, and Bryce. Carlotta took out her kettles, her mixing bowls and pans. She had cooked for her brothers in Wisconsin, and she was glad to cook for Bryce now. She made new recipes and old ones. She served Nebraska beef and Wisconsin cheese. Carlotta learned that she loved the things her mother had loved and even the things her grandma had loved when growing up in Pennsylvania. She loved bread dipped in her soup, pickled eggs, oatmeal, and sweet tomato gravy. Bryce took salsa on his eggs at breakfast time, Nebraska style, but she loved ketchup on hers. She thought back to girlhood days, breakfast-time-at-home days. So of course she thought of cornmeal mush.

Cornmeal mush was a family treat. Carlotta had learned to make mush from her mother, who learned from her mother. Carlotta's grandmother had grown up Amish, and she had learned to eat cornmeal mush.

It doesn't sound pretty, and your friends may think it's weird. But if you try it, you may find you are just like Carlotta and her brothers—you like it so much that you don't even mind cleaning up the huge Pie Lady mess!

Mush is the perfect thing to serve on a cool fall morning after you come in from feeding the chickens or milking the cow.

Or maybe you just got up early and sat out on the patio watching the sun rise.

Carlotta doesn't have much time for things like patio sunrises, these days. The baby came and the days are filled with things she has to do. And that's okay—as long as she isn't stuck in the house dusting or something on a perfectly gorgeous day. Carlotta dips her bread in her soup, and she thinks of cornmeal mush. Someday Bryce might like it too. Maybe sometime when they are visiting family in Wisconsin—some cold winter morning around the table during some Christmas trip, maybe—it will be just the perfect thing, topped with the perfect tomato gravy.

Meanwhile, Carlotta gets steaks ready to grill. She picks up her small daughter and grabs a minute to step outside. Together they watch the sun set behind the Nebraska hills. It's a good place, Nebraska. It's a good life here, a good place to make a home.

Here is the recipe for cornmeal mush, and as Carlotta's grandpa would say:

"It'll stick to your ribs!"

CORNMEAL MUSH

4–4½ quarts water
4 cups finely ground roasted cornmeal
1 tablespoon salt

In a large saucepan, bring 2 quarts water to a boil.
Separately, put cornmeal in an 8 cup measure. Add
2 quarts water, slowly mixing it with a whisk until all is
mixed well. Add to boiling water, stirring well. Add salt.
Cook on low for 30–60 minutes. Pour into a 9 x 13-inch
pan or into two or three bread pans. Refrigerate overnight.
(Here is where you sneak a bowlful, add brown sugar, and
have yourself a snack.)

When set, cut into ½-inch (or thinner) slices. Fry in plenty of
hot oil or lard until nice and crispy on both sides. Serve with
tomato gravy, thinly sliced onions, and a fried egg on the
side for a top-notch breakfast! Can't be beat!

Tomato Gravy

1 pint tomato juice or stewed tomatoes
2 tablespoons flour
2 tablespoons granulated sugar
¼ cup or more water

Bring tomato juice or stewed tomatoes to a boil.
Separately, make a thickening of the flour, sugar, and
water to make a thin paste. Add to the boiling tomato liquid. Boil a little to thicken; serve over hot fried mush.

19

Doing Good

LETHA

Whatsoever thy hand findeth to do, do it with thy might.

—ECCLESIASTES 9:10

"**P**ERFECT COUNTRY." Those were the words Kansas settlers sent to their family back east. "Perfect country," where
there are no stumps to dig out, no rocks coming up in the fields.
No water either, but that nobody mentioned. Letha's family
came to try this country. It suited them fine. They found plenty
of work to do under the open sky.

Merle came too, came from California, a young man on his
own. Letha married Merle and they started their own farm.
Wheat grew out in the fields, and so many other things grew
too: broiler chickens, cucumbers, children, trees. Water things,
tend them, face the sun and wind.

Perfect country.

The family grew. They grew up and left home. Day after day, Letha did the work in front of her. The roads are straight out here and the work was there in her hands—a pie to bake, the chickens to feed, the pickles to can. Many an evening when her granddaughter ran down the road and into the yard, she found Merle hoeing in the garden and Letha in a chair nearby, a big bowl of produce in her lap. To Letha's granddaughter it looked so easy, and it looked fun too. It looked like a good place to be while the sun went down and the wind played with the trees.

Merle grew things, and Letha worked with the harvest. Green beans, rhubarb, sand plums, cabbage, grapes. Or butchering days, which are another type of harvest. Letha taught her granddaughter to clean the chicken gizzards and how to clean out the intestines of the pig to use for sausage casing. After the butchering day, Letha would can headcheese and cracklings and sausage. Whatever it was that her hands found to do, she did it.

My mom remembers that not long after she and Dad were married, they were invited to Merle and Letha's house for Sunday dinner. Mom was young, and new to Kansas, and she loved the feeling of family at Merle and Letha's. Letha made a great dinner, but Mom's favorite part was the dessert. Letha made desserts, of course (her daughters love to remember the homemade tapioca pudding), but that day she hadn't gotten around to it. So she just frosted some graham crackers and set them on a plate. Mom loved it—it felt like home, eating frosted graham crackers there at Letha's table.

Have you ever made frosted graham crackers? Melt butter, add powdered sugar, milk, and vanilla. Add cocoa if you are a chocolate fanatic. Stir. If the frosting is too stiff, add more milk. If it's too thin, add more powdered sugar. Keep on until it's just the way you like it. Children love making frosting like this—sometimes they end up with a lot, and sometimes a little, but it's always good.

When the frosting is ready, break a graham cracker in half and spread it with frosting. Top it with the other half of the graham cracker. It's perfect snacking, and it isn't some grand and fancy recipe. That's why Mom felt that Letha's house was home.

What is home, really?

Clean clothes. A vacuumed floor. Goulash for lunch, fried bread *platz* with honey, cornbread and gravy, ham and bean soup. Going home means knowing what to expect, knowing the pickles have that slice of onion just under the lid, smelling the honey chicken when you walk in the door and knowing exactly what it will look like and how it will taste. It's that milk and dumpling soup, the one the family still calls "our soup" half a lifetime later. It's the people around the kitchen table.

Those were the days, those early days when Merle and Letha first came to Kansas. There was still ground to break, fields to plan, a way of life to make. Not many houses dotted the horizon—neighbors were few and important, and there was work for everyone. The years passed, the neighbors came, the town grew. The children grew up, Merle retired, but there was still something to do. Merle planted a garden, and Letha canned, and she cooked and baked and cleaned. She fried chicken for potlucks, made popcorn for snacking, invited the neighbors for coffee.

We have a tradition at church, in our home congregation where Letha and I spent many years together. Whenever anything special happens—if a family moves in, if someone plans to move away, if we have a special meeting, or if the new schoolteachers have arrived—we do something called "snacks after church." Those days, we each bring a plate of goodies, and after Sunday evening service we go downstairs and have coffee and cookies together.

One evening when we had snacks after church, I tasted some popcorn I really liked. It was too light to be caramel popcorn, but not soft and marshmallow-y either. It was light-colored, sweet, a little hard and a little soft, nutty, rich, and good. It was in a green Tupperware bowl. It was so perfect I went back for a second helping.

The next time we had snacks after church, there was the same popcorn in the same bowl. After that, every time we had snacks after church, I would scan the table for that green bowl, and it was always there. Once I saw Letha taking the bowl home, so I knew it was hers.

Finally I called her and told her how much I liked it. "Oh, that's just Crazy Crunch," Letha said. She gave me the recipe. "Do you know how to string syrup?" she asked.

"Yes, I have done that before," I said.

"Okay," she said, "just be sure you wait until it strings. It will take pretty long, maybe fifteen minutes. You know how to hold your spoon up over the kettle?"

"Yes," I said. "Yes, I can do that. Do you cook it fast or slow?"

"Oh, not too slow," Letha said. "And just until it strings."

I make Crazy Crunch now, even though I don't have a green Tupperware bowl. And I particularly like to watch the syrup string. You let it boil a few minutes, and then every minute (or less, but I do it over and over) you check it by getting a spoonful of syrup, holding your spoon up high, and pouring it slowly back into the kettle. At first it just pours. After a few minutes it falls off the spoon in globs. Keep going, and a few minutes later, it pours out of the spoon in a nice thin string. Try it; it really is fun. You take it off the heat immediately when it strings.

The work in front of you, that's the thing you have to do. Make several jars of dill pickles when someone brings in cucumbers. Shred some cabbage for sauerkraut. Roll out a batch of noodles. Bake a pie for dinner. Mix red hots and peanuts for the friends who stopped in this evening.

Some days things go well. Someone milks the cow and brings in the milk and you separate the cream and make the butter, placing it in its own wooden box. Other days you pour the cream into the separator and the whole thing flies apart, discs and cream going everywhere. Oh well. Maybe that's the day you accomplished a washed off wall and floor. After all, you can do your work on any kind of a day, one thing at a time. You can grow old, and you can say with a smile, "I'm doin' good."

Of course you are, you're doing good—one counter of pickles or sausage, one pan of fried chicken, one bowl of Crazy Crunch at a time. And wherever you are, even if it's here where the water is as rare as the trees, wherever your hands have work to do, that is your perfect country.

I'm doin' good.

CRAZY CRUNCH

2 quarts popped popcorn
1 ⅓ cup pecans
1 ⅓ cup almonds
1 ⅓ cup granulated sugar
1 cup butter
½ cup light corn syrup
1 teaspoon vanilla extract

Mix popcorn and nuts. In saucepan, combine sugar, butter, and corn syrup. Bring to a boil over medium (not low!) heat, stirring constantly. Continue boiling at least 15 minutes, or until it "strings." It will be a light caramel color.

Remove from heat and stir in vanilla. Pour over popcorn and nuts and mix well. Spread out on waxed paper until it cools, and then break apart and pile into a Tupperware bowl. (I am pretty sure that Letha used margarine in this recipe, but butter is always good.)

20

Choco-Cherry Comfort

ROSANNE

Feed me with food convenient for me.

—PROVERBS 30:8

ROSANNE TAUGHT SCHOOL for twenty-six years in eight different private schools across the United States and Canada. Some years she helped with small new schools, and other years she gave her best to older, established schools.

Teaching reading and writing while managing attitudes and attributes was big work. It was hard, it was good, and it took everything she had to give. Some days were better than others. Some days the children were ready to learn; other days it took extra thought and care. But hard or easy, bright or dim, Rosanne had a work to do, a chair and a desk to fill, a blackboard behind her and a marking pen before her, and a classroom full of children looking into her face.

In the summers, Rosanne went home and spent time with her parents. As they aged, she cared for them. And though she gave so much time and thought to her own work, many of her sweetest words are about her mom and her dad. Rosanne told me that the sound of love was like the sound of her mom greeting her at the door when she'd come home for the weekend from teaching school.

I can picture Rosanne driving up to her parents' place that weekend. I think maybe that week was a harder one, and I think maybe her mom even knew that. I can picture her mom, with a clean warm kitchen and a tall fresh cake.

And Rosanne opened the door and looked up the few steps toward the kitchen door. And the kitchen door opened, and there was Mom.

"Welcome home, Rosie," her mom says. "If I'd a-known you were coming, I'd a-baked you a cake!"

And Rosanne would see the smirk on her mom's face, and she knew just what her mom had baked for her that day.

When Rosanne's mom turned eighty-five, the family got together for a party. They baked her chocolate cupcakes, which she loves, and they swirled them high with bubblegum-pink frosting. They treated her with cards, roses, balloons, happy birthday songs, and lots of well wishes. There was bubblegum pink on every plate—and smiles on every face.

"Contentment is bubblegum pink," Rosanne wrote. "It tastes like a choco-cherry ice cream treat. It smells like fresh chocolate chip cookies just out of the oven."

Contentment means comfort and love. It means family and home. Yes, Rosanne, I agree—it's bubblegum pink and choco-cherry sweet. It's caring and sharing. It's Mom. It's a Pie Lady thing, fresh from the oven.

Rosanne's mom had a favorite cookie recipe she liked to share. These cookies are soft and sweet, old-fashioned and per-fect. Rosanne's mom always made them with chokecherry or chokecherry-and-rhubarb jelly. One of her friends uses rasp-berry jelly. I used jam I made from Kansas sandhill plums.

It was a satisfying thing to do, scooping cookie dough out of the mixing bowl, one tablespoon at a time. I loved scraping off the tablespoon to make them exact. I loved taking the time to roll each cookie nice and round and set it in its proper place on the pan. It was sort of fun to press an indentation (just so!) in each cookie with my thumb, and then to drop in a spoonful of jam. After ten minutes or so in the oven, the cookies were flat and perfect, buttery and oh-so-Kansas, with that tangy circle of sandhill plum. Pie Lady style, oh yes! It was the perfect way to spend a summer day.

They are Kansas or Manitoba, Minnesota or Pennsylvania. They are home, they are time, they are tangy and sweet. She could have named them Jelly Delights, but that wouldn't have improved them a speck. Cookies: that says enough for you to feel that you are home.

An open door says all I need to hear.

COOKIES

  1 cup butter
  1½ cup brown sugar
  2 eggs
  3 cups flour, or more if needed
  1 teaspoon cream of tartar
  1 teaspoon baking soda
  ½ teaspoon salt
  1 teaspoon vanilla extract
  Jam

Heat oven to 350°F. Cream together butter and brown sugar. Add eggs and mix well. Separately, sift together flour, cream of tartar, baking soda, and salt. Add to creamed mixture and mix well. Add vanilla; mix. Roll into balls. Make a depression in the center of each ball and fill with a rounded half teaspoon of jam. You could place a walnut on top instead of jam. Bake until golden brown, about 10 minutes.

21

All the Difference

EVIE

Let us choose to us judgment:
let us know among ourselves what is good.

—JOB 34:4

"**E**VIE," HER MOM said one day to the little girl in the middle of a houseful of children, "today is your birthday."

Her birthday! Of all her family, this day was hers, her very own. Evie loved the thought of it, and she never forgot the thrill of it. It was a detail, one of those details that makes something delightful.

Some of those details are worth working over—and over and over. Getting the pudding the right temperature for the meringue. Getting the proper number of tablespoons of water into the egg whites. Getting the right doll in the right place on the right stair.

Details can hang you up and drag you down, or they can brighten up your space and help you to forget about larger problems around you. The county may not have the money to pave the road you take to town. But your cookies are crispier today, and lighter, than the last time you made them. You may have too much or too little rain, or you may have a long, cold winter—but the aloe vera plant has a whole set of new leaves.

Details. Some you can focus on, some you have to forget. Invite a tableful of company and find a corner for yourself later. Cook up a stack of good things and claim a screened-in porch to use for your cooler. Fill the house with life, inside and out—vines covering the siding, plants holding up their leaves, family and friends sharing their ideas. Serve them your own regular Sunday dinner: they know what to expect, they know all their own favorite details, and you didn't have to plan what to put on the menu.

Details. Play with them, respect them, do what you like with them. Sing your own favorite song over and over, stretching the words and the music as you please. Leave the housework for today and read a story to a child. Read the story just the way you like it, all the words exciting, every phrase just so. And then? Do it again.

There's no need to try every new recipe, to chance-it-and-serve-it. Instead, take a recipe you know, make it well, and then make that dish again, following the same recipe more perfectly than you did before. And then? Do it again.

Follow the recipe, adjust according to your preferences. If the pudding ends up a little flat, round the ¼ teaspoon measure. But then remember and mark it down: "¼ rounded teaspoon salt." If the pie bakes too quickly, adjust the oven, and mark it down: now you will bake it at 345 degrees instead of 350.

You learn a lot by watching the details. You learn to fear a tablespoon of water, to worry what will happen when it meets your whipped-up egg whites. You learn the difference between cold water and warm, between warm and hot. You learn that a trip out to the garden or even off to the neighbor's is definitely worth it, as long as you end up with beautiful green-and-red stalks of rhubarb. And ultimately you may find yourself decked with a gorgeous rhubarb meringue, its peaks a mile (or so) high. It really is a Pie Lady moment.

Once Evie and her husband bought a secondhand oven. They installed the oven and set the cookbook that came with the oven up on the shelf. Years later, Evie took out that cookbook and started thumbing through the pages. She came across a recipe for meringue and stopped. She read it again.

It called for four egg whites, and sugar, and four tablespoons of water. Curious, Evie decided to try it. "But I've never had the nerve to try the four tablespoons!" she says. Then she laughs. "I use three."

It's a perfect fit for her rhubarb custard pie, because she uses four egg yolks in the custard, and four whites in the meringue.

Try it once and try it again. It takes time to make a masterpiece! Besides, your family will probably think your pie effort is a worthy cause. Someone may even say, someday, "These are the kind of flops I like." It's no secret that families love repeated experiments.

I love to make this meringue—it makes me smile, just to see it, not to mention how sweet and lovely it is to eat. Make sure your pudding is hot when you top it with the meringue. (Evie spent years getting that detail right; hot pudding works best!) Bake it until it is done, paying attention to your own pie in your own oven. Count your minutes, count your hours, and you will be ever so glad that you did!

Little things can make a big difference.

RHUBARB MERINGUE PIE

1 cup plus 2 tablespoons granulated sugar
½ scant cup flour (½ cup minus 2–3 teaspoons)
¼ slightly rounded teaspoon salt
½ cup heavy cream
½ cup water
4 egg yolks
3 cups finely diced rhubarb
1 (9-inch) pie shell, unbaked

Heat oven to 375°F. Mix sugar, flour, and salt. Add heavy cream and water. Add egg yolks, one at a time, stirring just until smooth. Add rhubarb. (Frozen rhubarb works well, but do not drain it as it thaws—add all the juice.) Pour into unbaked pie shell and cover edges of pastry with foil. Set your timer for 45 minutes; 5 minutes before it rings, jiggle the pie a little. When the pie is set, it is done. Take it out of the oven and remove foil. If making meringue, turn oven down to 350°F after you remove the pie.

MERINGUE

4 egg whites, just warmer than lukewarm (set your bowl
   in warm water for a few minutes)
¼ slightly rounded teaspoon cream of tartar
3 tablespoons barely lukewarm water
½ teaspoon vanilla extract
¼ scant teaspoon salt
½ cup granulated sugar

Beat egg whites, cream of tartar, and water until very
soft peaks form. Add vanilla. In a separate bowl, combine
salt and sugar, then add gradually to softly peaked egg
whites, whipping until stiff-but-not-too-stiff peaks form.
Watch carefully—as soon as you lift the beater and the
whites make a peak, stop beating. Pile the meringue on
the baked custard pie, touching edges of the pastry. Bake
15–17 minutes on lowest shelf of 350°F oven until meringue
is lightly browned.

22

Petunias and Other Good Things

HELEN

The Lord shall open unto thee his good treasure.

—DEUTERONOMY 28:12

IN A SMALL white house along a gravel road, Helen lived with her husband and three children, a boy and two girls. Day after day, year after year, she tended her house and her garden, her shopping and laundry. The garden took a lot of time, planting and weeding and tending. You watch for bugs and disease, you pull a weed. You walk out in the evenings just to see how things are coming.

You check to see if the leaves on the pink petunias are really as green as they should be. You deadhead the roses, you mix up some spray, you fertilize and water and weed.

Through all the busy days and years, there have been dresses to sew and fruit to can, windows to clean and errands to run.

There are quilts to plan and cut and piece and mark, hours of quilting to accomplish. But the thing Helen does, the thing Helen did, is make good things to eat.

It wasn't that Helen read all the cooking magazines or learned to make fancy things. It wasn't that she was thinking of the science behind the recipe or always finding new ways to cook. It was just that mealtime came around regularly, people came in to sit around the table, and Helen turned to her freezer and her pantry and had that table ready for dinner. It worked, too, absolutely. The children cleaned their plates and asked for more. They grew up, they made their own lives, but they always love to go back to that same table.

"We're going to Grandpas' for dinner," her married grandchildren tell their friends.

"Your Grandma makes good food," the friends say.

She does.

Potatoes, carrots, peas, buns, roast, a fresh chocolate cake. Each dish made in the way she has made it, over and over, perfect and comforting and good. It's what a mom does, it's the thing a grandma plans her week around, when the table is stretched out long and the places are set and the chairs are filled. The roast is tender, and the carrots and peas steam up in the quiet room. The buns are soft and white and ready for butter and jam. You're glad to go, you're glad for the food, and for some reason you feel happy.

Maybe it's the things that make you happy. What if it is? If it is—if all it takes is a pink petunia or a perfect loaf of bread— then it's easy be rich and happy, and the world belongs to you.

So many days are draggy or cloudy or stressful or sad. But on the dullest day, a rose is still a deep dark red, butter is still yellow on a blue plate, and flour still heaps up white on a sil-ver spoon. You might be tired this morning, but yeast bubbles and grows when you sprinkle it over water and chunked-up potatoes roast to crispy-edged brown. You might have a worry nagging at your mind, but the buttered peas look lovely in that bowl and the buns have perfect, flaky tops in all their softness.

If it's things that make you happy, you have it made. Your hands can make things, care for things, prepare things. It doesn't take more than a heap of petunias, a border of roses, or the smell of the flowers at sunset. If it's things that make you happy, if you feel surrounded by riches, you can enjoy the things that really matter—the guests around your table, each in the place you chose for them (just the right group for a few hours' conversation), the love you feel and the faith you share.

It's things like flowers and food that fill life with goodness, but it's also prayers, of course—prayers and love that keep a heart soft and keep light in a face. Good things and good times build up over all the years of practice. Once again, the roast, the cake, and the tall white buns. Once again, you go over the list: guests and food, menus and conversations.

You do it once: you clean your house and make the food and invite your friends. You make a dinner, make a conversation, make a friend. You spend your week in a quiet way cleaning your house, tending your roses, working at your quilt or in your kitchen. Then you do it again: clean your house and call your friends. And the friends are glad to come and glad to share, and the food is hot and good.

Good things, good times, good work for our hands to do.

HELEN'S BUNS

1 ½ cups water
2 teaspoons salt
8 tablespoons granulated sugar
1 ½ cups warm water
Several additional teaspoons granulated sugar
2 tablespoons yeast
3 eggs
Enough flour to make a soft dough (about 8 cups)
¼ scant cup lard, melted
¼ scant cup butter, melted

Heat 1 ½ cup water until boiling, add 2 teaspoons salt and 8 tablespoons sugar. Mix well and set aside to cool.

Mix warm water, additional sugar, and yeast. Let mixture sit until it bubbles. Then add to lukewarm water and eggs. Mix well.

Pour mixture into a large bowl. Add several cups of flour.

Add lard and butter. Beat well with a wooden spoon. Add more flour, alternately with stirring, until you need to start punching by hand. Go by feel. Make a soft dough. You don't want it too stiff.

Let rise in a warm place for 30 minutes. Punch down again, and then, when risen nice and high, form and let rise again in pans until ready to bake (about 30 minutes).

Bake at 400 or 425°F for 15 minutes, or until done.

23

Trifles and Stars

MARJORIE

So teach us to number our days,
that we may apply our hearts unto wisdom.

—PSALM 90:12

TALL BLUE CABINETS: that's what they remember. Blue cabinets and books on the bookshelves and a lamp's soft glow in the window. Violets out in the garden and stepping stones. Scrapbooks, pages of pictures and poetry, a game around the table, and fruit just picked from the tree.

The grandchildren love to think back over days at Grandma's, as grandchildren always do. Well, yes, they did have dinners there, and peppernuts to eat, and just-made jars of jam. They stopped at Grandpa and Grandma's for snacks after evening church services, so they remember cookies too, and cheese, and pepperoni. And they went for birthday parties, so there must have been cake— yes, definitely there was birthday cake and ice cream.

They ate ice cream there, they all agree, lots of times. It was perfect, that ice cream, mixed just right at the tall blue cabinets and frozen to perfection by Grandpa. They loved to watch him, his long arms turning the crank on the ice cream freezer. They ate the ice cream plain, with a side of saltine crackers. Ice cream, yes. They know they ate ice cream.

But otherwise? Really, exactly what they ate hardly matters. They didn't care then, and they don't care now. There's something they go to Grandma's house for—have gone for all these years—and really it's not the food.

It's a kitchen table. It's somebody waiting for you. It's an open door.

Always Grandma is at the door, clapping her hands. "Well, look who's here!" she says. Then you are in the door, with Grandpa smiling there by the bookcase and his great big chair. Well, look who's here, just past the violets, in where the lamps are lit.

That lamp, just like the door, asks you to come in. And it's Grandma's hands that keep the bulbs ready so the window is always bright. It's a trifle, the light bulbs. A trifle, the violets. A trifle, that clap of hands at the door. Grandma knows something, and she knew it long ago: trifles are tremendous.

Before Grandma was a grandma she was Marjorie, a young mom with ideas and ideals. She waited for children and welcomed them at last. Then she found herself trying to live out her ideals in the middle of stacks of everyday work. All around her, her friends were the same, working away at mountains of ordinary. They were too busy and there was too much to do, too many things to keep up with.

But if she looked, Marjorie could see bright moments on an ordinary day. It was amazing how those moments made everything worthwhile. It's the little things, she realized, that made her days worth living. Her husband's magazines beside his favorite chair. A smile for the child there beside you on her own special blanket. A story, a laugh, an apple (for a treat) without a peeling. Children loved small things, and she knew it. They loved to collect small treasures—shiny rocks, an old key, a pretty feather. They loved to have their very own box to keep those treasures in.

Marjorie thought and dreamed while she worked. Those little things, they mattered. Bright little moments made life sparkle. Sweet little moments needed compliments and praise. Bad little tendencies must be weeded out. Special little finds from a flea market or a sale made the house look like home.

Marjorie dreamed and prayed. Finally, her heart full, she started to write. She scribbled sentences at the table as she worked. She wrote in quiet moments, and she wrote at night. She finished a lovely slim book full of ideals and advice for her daughters and her friends. Trifles, Marjorie wrote, are tremendous. Take time for them.

Life was tremendous too. Ideals are stars, Marjorie found, and though you aim for them, you do not reach them. Of course you never reach them. You are only one mom, after all—one mom who wishes she could do all the things she meant to do. You make lunch and have a mess to clean up. You spend hours over a sickbed and fall into your chair, exhausted. You talk to your teenager and only hope they understand. Sometimes, in fact, they do not understand. You share your joys, you share your enthusiasm, you share your burdens and your sorrows.

And yet.

And yet! The children grew up and went off to their own homes. Grandchildren ran in and out of the house, day after day. Marjorie cooked for them, took them out to the orchard, served them snacks and tea. And they remember the blue cabinets, the violets, the lamp, and their grandpa's big tall chair. They remember, and they turn their steps toward that dear old open door, where they know Grandma is waiting.

There will probably be a cup of tea in an old china teacup, or peppernuts, or cheese, or a jar of homemade jam. They really don't worry about trifles like that when the door is open and two dear people are waiting. "Well," Grandma says, "look who's here!"

Because trifles are tremendous.

HOMEMADE ICE CREAM

8 eggs
1 cup brown sugar
1 cup granulated sugar
1 (14-ounce) can sweetened condensed milk
1 quart half-and-half
2 teaspoons vanilla extract
1 teaspoon salt
Milk

Beat eggs well, gradually add brown sugar and granulated sugar, and beat until thick and sugar is dissolved. Stir in sweetened condensed milk, half-and-half, vanilla, and salt. Pour into ice cream freezer and fill with milk until freezer is approximately two-thirds full. Put the dasher in the freezer and the lid on the top and set it in the freezer bucket. Then layer the bucket with ice and about 3 cups ice cream salt. Freeze according to your freezer's instructions. Makes 6 quarts.

24

The Trees and the Hills

MARSHA

And the hills shall break forth before you into singing.

—ISAIAH 55:12

SOMEWHERE OUT ON the Great Plains many centuries ago, Native Americans built grassy homes along a steep slope up above a creek. The winds blew. The sun shone every day, in the heat and in the cold. Some years there was plenty of meat and plenty of rain. Some years the dust blew and food was scarce. But there on the slope women cooked their food and tended their fields and their families. They looked out at the sun at the end of the day—sitting with their sons, perhaps, with the work behind them and the night coming on.

The centuries passed, and the people left their homes behind and moved on. In those ancient times no one wrote a history, so no one knows what threatened them. Only pieces of pottery and slight marks of houses lie buried under the sand.

And over the empty houses, the winds blew, the sun shone, and grasses grew with the seasons. Hawks dived and flew over the waving grasses.

The years rolled on. Maybe some years there were tepees dotting the grass beyond the slope. Maybe occasionally a group of hunters rode through. Season after season, the slope and the creek remained empty with only the call of the birds and the whisper of the grasses under the open sky.

Then wagons rolled in and the settlers came to this country they called new. The low rolling hills around it were sprinkled with houses and fields and fenced off into pastures. One day, a wagon pulled up to the top of a low hill. It stopped, and a man leaned out, looking. He could see north and south and east and west. Yes, this was the place. He claimed that hill, tamed it and worked it. The years rolled by until he too was gone and only hawks dived over the grasses.

At last one day, just as the sun set behind that hill, a Model T truck pulled in from the east and people piled out. The family was home.

Four generations later, Marsha and her husband moved to the place on the low hill. The ground rolls away from her log home, and you can see miles in every direction. Sometimes in the evening she sits at the door with her son. And the boy dreams of the days to come, and all that he will be and do, and Marsha dreams too. But she dreams of the days behind her, far away in the north among the trees.

Marsha was a girl who loved the woods. The woods behind her house had stood for hundreds of years, strong and change-less there behind the old-fashioned white farmhouse she called home. She loved to play in the shelter of the woods, loved the damp smell of the earth in the air and the crunch of leaves under her feet. The trees whisper old, old secrets. They stand firm and strong above you when you are small and trembling. They clap their hands in the breeze and are filled with the song of birds. If you listen, you may hear a whisper of their praise and the murmur of their laughter. There in the trees was the perfect place to play and dream.

Sometimes Marsha and her friends would build a bonfire in the woods and sit around the fire, singing songs and dreaming dreams. Some dreams you could whisper to each other, but some were sacred, a tiny glimpse into a glorious eternity. Those nights the sky was close, and there, just past the trees, so close that you could feel the pull, you felt the presence of God. You could trust and dream and know that heaven is real and God is good.

Marsha grew up. She married the man she loved, left the farmhouse and the woods, and made a new home on a ranch on the rolling plains. Marsha missed the dear old trees, but sometimes she felt the pull of the wide and empty hills.

Today Marsha is far from the whisper and the laughter of the woods. Life is full of appointments and work and is marked with partings and sorrows. Although of course the busy days mean that love is all around, and partings make heaven near.

It's the pull of heaven that makes you hear the song of heaven around you. It's the chill of fall that makes you sit close around the fire. You can sit in the kitchen watching the rain, chili on the table and the family all around you. You can look at the sky and feel the strength and the nearness of God. You can sit with friends around the fire down at the creek, where the water hides down in the rocks. Like those mothers and sons of long ago, you need a fire by the creek, a place to eat your food under a wide and starry sky.

Across the hill, if you listen closely, you might hear a sweet old song. The strength of the hills sounds so much like the laughter of the trees. And in the home against the hill, there's dinner waiting, work almost done, and a book to read. There are flowers on the step, a light in the window, and bread just baked, or a pie.

And somewhere beyond the hill, the steep old slope holds a thousand dreams where mothers and sons sat in the sun, the day's work behind them. And the people are gone but hope and love live on. The centuries roll on, sure as the sun. Today the sun shines on a new log home with its work and its play, its light in the window, its sorrows and joy. But a hawk still dives through the clouds and above the grasses, and underneath are the everlasting arms.

Spring always comes again.

CHILI

1 pound ground beef
1 medium onion, chopped
½ teaspoon minced garlic
1 cup fresh diced tomatoes OR 1 8-oz. can tomato sauce
1 (15-ounce) can pork and beans
1 (15-ounce) can black beans
1 (15½-ounce) can Southwest-style pinto beans
½ (4-ounce) can diced green chilies
1 (10¾-ounce) can tomato soup
3 cups water
1 teaspoon ground cumin
1½ tablespoon chili powder
1½ teaspoon salt
½ teaspoon pepper

In a large saucepan, fry ground beef with onion and garlic. Add remaining ingredients and heat through. If you double the recipe, you can add a larger variety of beans (such as Great Northern beans and kidney beans) and make it even more colorful and tasty. And it only gets better as you simmer it—try simmering it 2 hours, and you won't be sorry!

25

Big Sister, Little Sister

DEANNA AND CHARIS

Two are better than one;
because they have a good reward for their labour.

—ECCLESIASTES 4:9

IT WAS TOO bad, Deanna thought, for such a teeny-tiny little sister to be so sick. Deanna remembered her turn at chicken
pox. She remembered how she hated the itch, how badly she
wanted to scratch the awful spots.

Poor little Charis and her flushed little face and her small
spotty arms! Deanna took up the lotion bottle and rubbed the
little arms lightly. Really, it was fun to have a sister thirteen-
and-a-half years younger than you. Too bad Charis was too big
to rock now. Deanna pushed the hair out of Charis's flushed
face and watched her relax. Then she went off to work.

It was a special thing, having a small sister. Charis always
made Deanna smile. Some days you would find her behind

the curtains in the bay window, gazing up to the sky as if she were watching for angels. The next day you would find her in the same spot, letting all the dollies have it over how very noisy they were in church. And then the next day she would be way out in the trees, busy, full of importance in her special hidden house.

Once Charis came running, her face full of tragedy. "My dolly! My dolly!" Charis cried. "She's drowning!" Deanna ran after Charis. There was poor dolly, water dripping from her head. "I was giving her a drink!" Charis could hardly talk for crying. "I was only giving her a drink, and now she's drowning!"

Deanna grabbed a thick towel and dried the doll until not a drop of water was in sight. She placed her on the folded towel to dry and rest. She did like helping Charis. It didn't take much. In an hour or so or a day or two, Deanna could design a wardrobe for the entire doll family. It was fun to surprise her little sister, and it didn't take much, really. Charis was so often alone. Deanna remembered days when she too had wished for a friend. She remembered moments that made her understand what "alone" felt like. It made her want to do something for Charis. After all, she knew how long loneliness could feel.

Sometimes it took only a few minutes—just enough to cut a few extra things from the catalog to make the house or the church or whatever Charis was playing a little more real. Sometimes it took a few more minutes—time to draw a paper doll or a dress for her, time to trace an already-colored coloring book picture. Charis sat at Deanna's elbow and watched breathlessly while Deanna drew. It was fun.

Such a dear little sister, with her two little braids and her bright red shoes, running off to school excited, and running home again. Such a funny little sister, full of importance, with such huge ideas and problems in grade one. Such a precious little sister, at her elbow while she made a Donald Duck birthday cake for a friend. Just watching Charis watch her, Deanna knew the cake was a success.

Charis grew bigger and hung around Deanna whenever she could, watching, listening. All too soon, Deanna got married and moved away from home. She smiled at the clouds in Charis's eyes when she looked at Ken, but it made her throat hurt too. Poor, dear little sister! She couldn't understand how exciting it was for Deanna to be marrying him. She only knew that Ken planned to take her sister away. Deanna talked to her mom and convinced her that Charis should wear a big girl dress for that wedding day, complete with a stiff belt around her waist. She was quite grown up now, really.

Charis loved to visit Deanna. She carefully touched Deanna's projects—each piece of copper punching, macramé, crocheting, quilting, painting, embroidery, and cross-stitch. And some days, Deanna came and spent the day at home. She would work on her projects, and sometimes she would also sew a new dress for Charis or her doll.

As Charis grew, she wanted bigger things, like a bridesmaid's dress. And finally, she even wanted advice. Because Charis was teaching school now. Her difficulties now were much greater than a drowning dolly. Deanna could still listen, and give ideas, and try to understand.

When Charis got married after seven years of teaching, people called her capable, but she was still Deanna's little sister. She called Deanna when she needed advice or ideas. She called her when food didn't turn out right. It was fun to be doing the same work, in the same way, each in her own place.

Dear little Charis, Deanna thought, though of course now she didn't say it. Charis was taller than she was, now, and she might not understand.

The years swing by. Charis now has her own daughter to love and train. That daughter came, a precious little person straight from God, in answer to a prayer. But Charis still calls Deanna, asking how and what and when.

"You do it so perfectly," Charis says. "You do a big project and look—just as good as ever, not a hair out of place. But me! Look at these perennial beds! They will never look like yours."

Deanna looks at her sister, standing in front of her home, her small daughter running in and out. She laughs and gives in, offering advice on little fixes here and there. But she loves the way it looks, just the way it is. She loves sitting with Charis in her yard, looking at her thick, abundant tomatoes. If Deanna wants to grow tomatoes, she calls Charis for advice. Of course she does! That's what sisters do.

"You do things just right," Charis says. "That bread you make, such perfect cinnamon rings." She thinks of walking in the door at her sister's house and smelling cinnamon. It's a perfect thing on a cool fall day—it's not a new candle, it's the real thing.

Such a perfectly dear little sister. Deanna looks up from the tea Charis handed her, the perfect cookie on the plate, and smiles. "I'll give you the recipe," she says.

A sister is the best kind of friend.

PERFECT CINNAMON BREAD

2 cups milk

¼ cup lard

½ cup granulated sugar

4 teaspoons salt

½ cup instant potato flakes

2½ cups lukewarm water

2 tablespoons instant yeast

6–7 cups bread flour (Gold Medal Better for Bread
brand is preferred), divided

2 cups whole wheat flour

In a microwave-safe bowl, heat milk, lard, sugar, and salt
until lard melts, about 4–5 minutes. Add potato flakes and
water. Cool to lukewarm. Separately, stir yeast into 2 cups
flour and add to milk mixture. Add whole wheat flour. Stir
on low speed of mixer and slowly add remaining flour.
Knead dough on lightly floured surface and let rise until
doubled in bulk, about 1 hour.

Heat oven to 400°F. Divide dough into four sections and roll
out on lightly floured (or greased) counter. Roll each piece
into a strip 6 x 21 inches. Sprinkle with cinnamon sugar (see
below). Roll up and seal ends. Place in four 4 x 8-inch loaf
pans and let rise until almost doubled, 20–30 minutes.

Place pans in oven and turn down to 350°F. Bake
30 minutes. The loaves come out with slightly floury tops:
soft, whole grain bread with cinnamon rings—enjoy!

CINNAMON SUGAR

⅔ cup granulated sugar
4 tablespoons ground cinnamon

Stir together in small bowl.

26

It's a Friend Thing

DELILAH

I thank my God upon every remembrance of you.

—PHILIPPIANS 1:3

DELILAH GREW UP in California with her dad and her mom and her sisters and brother. She had good times at school with her friends and fun times on the bus ride home. She watched the landmarks as they were going home—the curve around the Blueberry Hill restaurant; the two palm trees that marked the exact center of California, the Golden State; the train tracks where, on the very best days, she saw the little red caboose. But most of all, she loved when the bus pulled in at home, loved running in the front door and finding fresh white bread cooling on the counter.

"Mom!" Delilah said, dropping her lunchbox and books. "Can I have some?" The bread was still warm, and Delilah buttered her piece carefully. It was a home thing, that buttery after-school bread. It was a Mom thing, just like the apron Mom wore, like the songs she sang while her hands were busy. Mom smiled as Delilah ran in, and the smile had love and even friendship in it.

Friendship was everywhere, in so many dear familiar faces. Friendship ran ahead of her when the family went to Grandpa's for Christmas. It filled her heart with a bounce so that she could hardly keep still, sitting by Grandma in church. "Winning souls, winning souls, winning souls for Jesus," Grandma sang. Delilah squiggled to the side so she could look up and watch Grandma's face. Surely no one sang like Grandma. Surely no one had such a perfect grandma for a friend.

Delilah bounced through the days at Grandpa's, bounced up into the golf cart beside him for a ride. She bounced into the bed made for her on the living room floor, and she sat straight up when the cuckoo popped out of the clock with eight noisy "cuckoos" in the morning. Delilah tiptoed over to the breakfast table. Grandpa's teasing, Grandma's laughter, sausage and pancakes and stories and fun: friendship at its best. No, Grandpa, no, no *thanks*, no Meadow Fresh milk! Grandpa laughed as he offered it—he knew she *never* drank Meadow Fresh! Orange juice and sausage, devotions time and early morning—that was a Grandpa-and-Grandma thing, the riches of family and friends. Delilah could hardly hold still for all the happiness popping up around her.

Delilah grew up. Her friends called her Deli. She grabbed every chance she could to visit friends, go to weddings, drive off on weekend trips. She grabbed any reason and away she went. Friends, singing and laughing late into the night. Friends out shopping, grabbing lunch, friends playing ball. Friends talking, discussing, and even arguing about things that mattered and things that didn't. She loved her friends and the good things in her life. She loved the time she spent in Arizona caring for children whose parents could not care for them. It was good to be Deli.

Deli got married and moved to a new home at the edge of the Flint Hills of Kansas, where she could look out the window and watch the sunset against those hills. There, too, she found friends to laugh and talk and sing with, friends to worship and visit with, friends to share and advise in her new role of farm wife and the later joys and challenges of being a mom.

Deli's friends were near her when her almost-fourteen-month-old child suddenly and unexpectedly died. Then, oh then, Deli learned about the depths of pain and sorrow that are in this world! Her friends were near to take her out to eat or take her shopping. They were near with visits and comfort.

They were near, too, with help and new dresses when her next little baby was born sixteen weeks too early. They were near through the long hospital stay and they were near, smiling, when the baby finally came home. Ah, friendship! It's a great strength in this old world.

Not long ago, Deli and her husband and their four children took a trip to Alberta. It was in Alberta that Delilah learned about poutine, a Canada thing. Even the Albertans learned from their friends, because poutine began as a Quebec thing. Deli loved Alberta, loved all the Canadian things she saw and heard. She loved the cool, jackets-needed evenings, each one the perfect setting for a campfire. Those campfires were Canada at its best—Alberta sky above you, a soft thick sweater around you, a marshmallow on the stick in your hand, and friends all around you. Marshmallows, yes, stuffed between chocolate-covered crackers. Buffalo wings. Shrimp. That Canadian thing—poutine.

Poutine is fries—crisp fries, soft in the center, deep-fried if you can manage it, topped with cheese. But not just any cheese. Cheese curds: the newest, freshest cheese curds you can find, and topped with beef gravy—not too thick, of course. Light, peppery beef gravy poured at the last minute over the fries and cheese, just so the cheese starts to melt. You can eat the poutine as a side dish with steak if you like, steak grilled over a grate. Or you can top it with steak, with peppers and onions, or with sauce Bolognese. It's a Canada thing.

It was a long drive from Kansas to Alberta, but at the end of it there are friends. In the kitchen, someone's making gravy. In the yard, someone's cooking steaks on a grate over the fire. There's a baking sheet on the counter with fresh hot fries. There are cheese curds and gravy over the fries. There is teasing for the Americans, teasing back for the Canadians, and singing in the night with a flashlight to light the songbooks. Teasing, singing, chairs pulled in toward the fire. Friendship. And now Deli knows a thing or two about poutine.

Friendship. It makes the miles worthwhile. It touches all those lonesome achy places in a heart that is missing someone sweet and small. Friendship. We lift each other up. We see God over all.

Today, Deli makes white bread for her family. She makes pancakes and sausage, and she even makes poutine, the Canada thing. Fresh bread, a Mom-at-home thing. Pancakes and sausage, a just-like-Grandma thing. Good food and good times, a Pie Lady thing. And wherever you are, in the sun or the shade, if you look, my dear, you will see—it's a friend thing.

Friends know things.

POUTINE

> 1 large bag french fries, seasoned or not seasoned
> 2 (12-ounce) bags cheese curds (or tiny cubes of mozzarella cheese)
> beef gravy (leftover Sunday dinner gravy works well, or mix up gravy from a packet)

Bake french fries in oven according to package instructions. When they are crispy and hot, sprinkle generously with cheese curds. Finally, pour gravy over all and place back in oven just until the cheese is melted. Eat quickly before someone else has a chance to eat your share!

27

Dairy Life

POLLY

Beloved, let us love one another: for love is of God.

—1 JOHN 4:7

ONCE UPON A time there was a farm in Oklahoma, a dairy farm. Maybe you do not think of dairy farms when you think of Oklahoma, but they are there. Maybe even if you visited this farm in Oklahoma, you would not have thought much about the cows on the farm or the hours spent milking them. Because on this farm it was not only the cows that mattered.

On this Oklahoma dairy farm, a minister and his wife raised eight children. One of the girls in the middle of the family was named Lila. Lila smiled and laughed and learned to walk and run. Her dad watched her and he smiled too. "She looks like a Polly," he said. She did. She looked like a Polly, so they called her Polly. She was Polly on a dairy farm in Oklahoma. It was a busy life of farmwork, housework, many kinds of work.

Polly learned to milk cows. She learned to enjoy the outdoors, out in the milk barn, out by the pond, or under the trees. She learned how to drive a car before she was really old enough so that she could drive her mother the five miles to town every week to do the washing. They carried the stacks in dirty, ran the wringer washer, and carried them out clean. Then they did the weekly shopping and went back home. There Polly learned how to take care of people by helping her mother. For really, on that farm, it was not only the work that mattered.

Polly helped her mother help all kinds of people. Her little brother needed watching, the family needed supper, her dark-haired little sister needed someone to help her at the table, friends and neighbors needed snacks in the evening or Sunday dinner. Polly helped get ready for company. She saw the fun of the work and the goal of it, when Sunday after Sunday the table was full of people and good times and new ideas. She learned that her brother who needed special care was dear to her—but she never learned to call him "handicapped." The dairy farm in Oklahoma was a wide place.

The cows were cared for, of course, the house was comfortable, and the food was old-fashioned and good. Saturdays were good, with their finish of baked beans and bread. Even washing dishes was good, because she was washing them with her big sister, year after year, until suddenly her big sister was married and Polly was the big sister. Little sister, big sister, big talks, little things.

The little girl named Lila grew up. She was tall now, but she was still Polly. Every week, Polly cleaned a house in town for a wage of sixty-five cents an hour. After a few years, she got married and moved to Michigan where she lived on a farm—a dairy farm, it turns out. On this Michigan dairy farm, it wasn't only the cows that mattered, though the work was good. Polly still milked cows. She learned to drive tractor. She liked driving tractor, and she liked living on a farm near the beautiful Michigan woods. There were lakes to discover, tree-lined roads to drive, apples to pick, fish to catch, woods to walk in.

But it's the evenings that are the best—evenings that matter. No wonder we talk about "spending" evenings! Evenings—perfect, long evenings with people you care about—are riches. Day after day we get to decide how best to spend them.

Some evenings the young Michigan family went on a drive, all of them in the single cab pickup with a bottle of pop they all shared. Sometimes they ended up at the neighbors' place for a visit. Sometimes they stopped at Harold's Dairy Delight. Then it was fun to watch Polly's little girl eat her lemon ice cream cone. She always licked it carefully, making it last the whole ten miles home.

There were home evenings, beautiful outdoor evenings playing catch or shooting baskets. There were indoor evenings of Probe, Monopoly, Password, or Laura Ingalls Wilder—and many of those evenings topped with popcorn around the family table.

Polly has company over like her mom did—she cleans her house and she cooks old-fashioned food and new things too. She makes pies, of course, but she has learned other things: pizza on Saturdays, fried fish, baked venison, chocolate pudding cake, enchiladas with rice and sopapillas. She has made the enchiladas over and over, all through the years. They make a perfectly beautiful special supper or even a birthday supper. Often she tops off those enchiladas-and-sopapilla suppers with butterscotch pie.

Polly's family has always loved that supper—both on the picture-perfect pie nights and on the evenings when Polly wondered why the meringue seemed so weepy. Every time she made it, the family was sure it was scrummy and special and Pie Lady perfect. Besides, they had Probe to look forward to, or baskets to shoot, or a sunset drive. They had a table set, good food to eat, and people around the table. It was dairy life, farm life, a wide, lovely life, and it can happen in Oklahoma or Michigan or anywhere far or near.

Her dad was right—she is Polly. And as Polly learned back in Oklahoma, it's much more than the farm—more than the beans or the bread pudding or the meringue—that matters. It's not your name or your farm or your work that makes life good. It's people, and evenings, and the occasional butterscotch pie.

It's not the cows, my dear; it's people that matter.

BUTTERSCOTCH PIE

⅓ cup butter
1¼ packed cup brown sugar
¼ slightly rounded cup cornstarch
½ teaspoon salt
2¾ cups milk
3 egg yolks, slightly beaten
1½ teaspoon vanilla extract
1 (9-inch) pie shell, baked
Meringue (see p. 21)

Melt butter in saucepan. Mix brown sugar, cornstarch, and salt, and add to butter. Then add the milk and the egg yolks and cook over medium heat, stirring constantly, until mixture thickens. Remove from heat and stir in vanilla. Pour into baked pie shell, top with meringue, and bake at 350°F until meringue is done, about 20 minutes.

28

The Big Little Teaspoon

VALERIE

Ye are the salt of the earth.

—MATTHEW 5:13

VALERIE GREW UP Dutch. Oh, she was Canadian, of course; her grandparents came to Canada soon after World War II. Still, in many ways, through all the years, her family kept their Dutch traditions. The women were homemakers. They planted gardens. They ate pickled herring and baked with almond extract at Christmastime. Valerie's grandma loved to sew, and she always made soup and sandwiches for Sunday dinner.

Valerie was fourteen when she first volunteered at the soup kitchen with her dad. It was at the soup kitchen that she met the Mennonites she eventually claimed as her church home. The Mennonites pulled up to the soup kitchen in a mint-green van. No horse and buggy? Just a homely mint green van? Valerie wondered. She listened while a couple of tall, thin young men

THE BIG LITTLE TEASPOON • 163

read the Bible and then sang an old hymn. Valerie wasn't sure what to think about these Mennonites. She wasn't sure about the mint-green van, and she wasn't sure about their style of singing that hymn.

But still. Valerie's family and the Mennonites were each familiar with the soup kitchen. They each had a part in giving a fresh hot meal to those in need. And although Valerie didn't know it then, some of these Mennonites also had Dutch roots. Mennonite people left Holland many years before Valerie's family. They spent a century or two in Germany and another century in Russia before finally settling in America, where they joined other Mennonites from places like Switzerland. The women were homemakers. Many of them planted gardens and most of them sewed their own clothes. They made special Christmas dinners and baked with anise extract at Christmastime.

The years flew by, and before she knew it, Valerie was married and in her own Mennonite home. She loved her husband, her home, and all the new friends around her. She loved the old stories of Holland, but she also loved the Mennonite traditions. She and her friends were homemakers. They planted gardens and sewed. Sometimes it was amazing how much Valerie thought like her friends—how close to the same day they all headed out to the garden spot with seeds in their hands. In some ways the gardens were different, of course. Valerie planted kale in hers along with the spinach and lettuce. She planted a European green bean and sliced the beans French style instead of chunking Blue Lake beans into jars.

But after all, she is planting a garden, complete with beans. She makes toast for breakfast and bakes for Christmas—old family recipes with almond flavoring. She is one of the bunch, of course, baking and growing and keeping. It is comfortable, it is traditional, it is good. Her friends love to compare notes, to discuss everything from the newest recipe to the latest world event.

"I'm so vanilla," one friend said as the group took off on the latest grand idea. "I just want to stay home and bake bread and color with my children." Vanilla. And just then they were sitting together in this friend's living room. They had finished lunch and left the dishes stacked on the counter.

"We don't want to waste time doing dishes," the vanilla friend said. Well, of course not, my dear, why would we? The hours fly—hours spent talking and laughing over so many funny little things. Big things are everywhere: amazing philosophies and discoveries. But why should we care about expeditions and explorations, about birds or bridges or water towers? We're talking together, the children are adorable, and we need to plan supper. Life is good, life is sweet, as homey as vanilla.

Vanilla! Just the sound of it makes Valerie think of comforting foods like her friend's blueberry coffee cake. Her friend with her children and their crayons feels as comfortable as a busy, happy kitchen. Think of the toppings over all things vanilla, something warm and sweet and good. Pull a quilt up to your nose and think of the hours someone spent creating it. Spark up a hefty conversation with a tease and think of the comfort in sharing laughter. Spend a morning talking—just talking—and count the goodness in the hours. Wrap your arms around the comfort of vanilla goodness, wrap your heart around it, dear as dear.

It's funny sometimes, to think that when two friends are alike it's the differences that stand out. It's the half teaspoon of flavoring that changes a cake or a pie. The chocolate sprin-kles on the toast make it Dutch; the cinnamon sugar makes it Canadian. And yet—and yet—underneath the sprinkles, both pieces of toast are crusty and hot and soft, tasting of morning and home. One family bakes anise-flavored peppernut cook-ies at Christmas; one hunts for chocolate letters. But each of them has that excited, once-a-year feeling of expectancy and togetherness.

Almond extract or vanilla, it's only a teaspoon of difference. Either way, it's a home, it's a coffee cake, it's a breakfast, it's a break. It's the salt in the bread that makes it worth eating; it's the difference in a friend that makes her dear. The crumbs on your counter could tell a whole story of creating, of comfort and sharing. They might tell you something sweet about the last blueberry on the white plate or the tiny piece of coconut on a silver tray. Or they might only remind you that the strawberry shortcake you had for breakfast was a really great idea. That big little teaspoon is life at its best. It's Pie Lady good.

Don't forget the flavoring, my dear.

BLUEBERRY COFFEE CAKE

Cake
    2¼ cups flour
    1½ cup granulated sugar
    3 teaspoons baking powder
    1 teaspoon salt
    6 tablespoons butter, melted
    Milk (added to melted butter to make 1½ cup)
    1 egg
    1 teaspoon vanilla extract

Blueberry topping
    1½ cup blueberries
    2 tablespoons butter
    ¾ cup flour
    6 tablespoons granulated sugar

Preheat oven to 375°F.

Mix the cake: In a large bowl, mix together flour, sugar, baking powder, and salt. In another bowl, mix butter, milk, egg, and vanilla. Add to dry ingredients and mix well. Pour into a greased 10 x 15-inch pan.

Make the blueberry topping: Sprinkle blueberries on cake batter. Separately, cut butter into flour and sugar. Sprinkle over blueberries.

Bake for 30–35 minutes.

ALMOND SQUARES

Crust
    1 cup butter
    1 cup granulated sugar
    3 cups flour
    2 teaspoons baking powder
    4 egg yolks
    2 teaspoons almond extract

Topping
    4 egg whites
    ½ cup brown sugar
    ¼ cup granulated sugar
    1 teaspoon almond extract
    2 cups finely shredded coconut

Make crust: Mix ingredients well and press into 9 x 13 baking dish.

Make topping: Beat egg whites until stiff. Gradually add brown sugar and granulated sugar. Add almond extract. Fold in coconut. Pour over crust in baking dish.

Bake at 350°F for 35 minutes.

29

Perky and Peace (and Peas)

HULDA AND VELDA

*Trust in the Lord, and do good; so shalt thou dwell in the
land, and verily thou shalt be fed.*

—PSALM 37:3

AT EVENING, ON a quiet street, Dad parked the car. We
piled out, up the walk, and pushed open a door. Dad, Mom, we
three sisters and our little brother shrugged out of our jackets at
the foot of a narrow stairway. To the left, a tiny hallway ended in
a closed door; to the right, a birdcage with a furiously chirping
parakeet dominated the room where a grandma sat and rocked
in a chair with flat red cushions.

"Hi, Hulda," we said while she nodded and smiled and
held our hands in hers. Hulda's daughter Velda scurried
from the kitchen with welcomes for us and scoldings for the
parakeet.

"Perky," she insisted, "you be quiet now. Be quiet, Perky."

Dad watched with a slight raise to his eyebrows as Velda tapped at the cage, and Mom leaned close to Hulda, clasping her hand. We children scrambled down two steps to the toy room with its line of dolls. Velda rescued old dolls. Up in her room at the top of the stairs, she washed them and sewed them new clothes. She even fitted them out with wigs. We said hello, and the dolls stared back. Then we stepped down two more steps into Velda's office.

Velda was a nurse practitioner, a new thing in those days, and she had an office attached to the house. In the office we found a desk, a cot, and even a treadmill, something we had not seen anywhere else. Back and forth between the treadmill and the toy room we went, running and then caring for the large family of dolls. We could hear voices in the next room going up and down, mixed with Perky's nonsense and grownups' laughter. Finally we heard a clatter in the kitchen, and we arranged the dolls stiffly along their bench. Cautiously stepping up into the living room, we smiled at Hulda and saw Mom standing near the sink in the kitchen, waiting to help.

"Come here, you girlies," Velda called from an unseen place. "What kind of tea do you want tonight?"

We found Velda in the lovely clutter of the pantry, with its rows of cans and packages and the boxes of tea. The decision wasn't easy, and she carried them out to the counter under the hanging light so we could decide.

Velda took down the teapots and turned on the stove; we watched the blue flame of the burner, smelled the cinnamon-orange of the tea we'd chosen, and twisted on our stools until we heard the kettle sing out. In went the tea bags, click went the lid, and back into the pantry went Velda. We watched her pile her find onto the table; blond store-bought cookies we had never tried, crackers, a stack of napkins. We watched her slice kiwi onto a plate, and we studied the plastic net clothespinned to the curtain. Velda explained how she washed the nets the grapes came in, filled them with food for the birds, and set a doll out near it to keep the squirrels away.

Outside the window, a tree loomed close and tall. I could almost see Velda tying the filled net to the branches and calling, "Come here, all you birdies!" It did not surprise me to hear that she had seen a cardinal there, although cardinals are definitely not Kansas residents. If a cardinal flew through—if it looked for a friendly place to stop—I do think he would have liked Velda's net of seeds, and her tree, and even her birdie call.

Velda settled Hulda carefully into her chair at the table and filled a spoon with cookie bits. "Come here, Perky," she called. Dad turned and watched, eyebrows higher than before, as the sassy bird settled onto the table Velda had prepared for us and pecked away at the treat. Velda chuckled at Dad's strained laugh and told Perky to go now.

"That's all," she said to the bird, and to Dad she added, "I always get a clean spoon, you know—we don't share spoons."

Choosing a chair, Dad laughed again and sampled the cookies and the kiwi. We scooted in on our bench, watched Hulda's smiles, and listened to the conversation spark across the room.

We never sang those nights, though we usually sang wherever we went. Hulda didn't mind singing, but it wasn't necessary to her; she liked sitting in her chair, smiling and listening to other people's discussions. Once in a while Mom would ask her for a story, especially the one about how she and her husband had given their lives to the Lord. We leaned forward in our chairs while Velda took her turn nodding and smiling.

"Bill and I were young then," Hulda said, "and we weren't living right. I felt so bad, but just couldn't seem to change. Then one day I got so tired of it I prayed to the Lord, 'I am willing for anything, Lord, anything, whatever it takes to wake us up.'"

We held our breath. Slowly Hulda went on, "The next day I found our two-year-old son floating facedown in the stock tank. I knew right away why he had drowned. We changed our lives and lived for the Lord. I have never been sorry."

"But didn't you find it hard to accept your son's death?" my parents asked Hulda. "And weren't you afraid to say you were willing for *anything*?"

In the quiet room, Hulda slowly stirred her tea. The cuckoo stepped out of his door, waiting to chime the hour.

"Well," Hulda said, "I was willing for whatever it took. I wanted to be right with God." The cuckoo sprang into action, singing, while we thought of the story and read the lines on Hulda's face. You could see that Hulda believed God knew what he was doing. You could feel that she trusted that all things had worked for good for all of them. Our hearts ached, but Hulda's voice never wavered. Her face had a sweet light.

When someone who has lost so much says something like that, you listen. There is no way you can imagine it and nothing you can say.

"I just love the Lord," Hulda said.

Discussions buzzed around that room while Perky scolded, darting in and out. Always Hulda smiled, and sometimes she said a word or two that made complicated things simple again. She told the story of her children's friend, the boy who called their house one day; he knew her children, but didn't know her name and didn't know what to say when she answered the phone.

"Hello—Mom?" he said.

"Yes," Hulda answered. After all, she *was* Mom there. They laughed together and she invited him over for watermelon.

We children drank our tea, those nights, and then slipped back to the treadmill or out to the backyard and its medley of growing things. We always closed doors behind us, and Perky dashed about the house, his reign unquestioned. He settled on Velda's shoulder or even the top of her head, just in the center of her wavy gray hair.

One day a man came to sit with Hulda, a man who had faced many sorrows. Hulda listened to him, and Velda served snacks and tea, and the man left happy. He came again. Before long, the phone rang at our house.

"Velda's getting married!"

We hurried over, up the walk and through the door, to Hulda rocking in the chair and Velda in the kitchen. When we circled around Hulda, Velda joined us; we congratulated her and heard the wonderful story of her betrothal.

"What will *you* do, Hulda?" Mom asked.

"Oh," Hulda said, "I am going to the rest home. I've told Velda she has done her part for me."

We could not picture the quiet grandma in the bustle of the care home. But she looked so cheerful about it that we didn't say a word.

"What will happen to Perky?" we asked.

"Perky flew out the door the other day," Velda said. "He isn't here anymore."

It was then that we noticed the quietness of the room, and we looked at Velda with amazement. How could Velda have left a door open, after all these years? The talk and the plans went on. Like Perky, Velda stood at a door that had opened after long years. Soon she would leave the life she loved for a larger one.

The bridal shower passed, the wedding happened, and Velda went away with her husband. The old house was emptied and sold. Hulda spent a couple of quiet, happy years in the care home before she slipped away to the Home she'd prepared for so long ago, the place where her baby and her husband awaited her.

We thought of Velda and wondered if she served tea to friends in her own new home, filling hours with ideas and conversation. Months stacked into years, and Raymond and Velda came back for a visit. Taller now, but still tea-party fans, my sisters and I went to say hello.

"We had such good times at your place," I said. "I love to remember them."

"Ray, these are Jewel's girls," Velda said while she held our hands in hers. She smiled and nodded, and I thought of Hulda, and saw a familiar light shining from Velda's face.

Sometimes these days I get into buzzing, anxious discussions. What should be done, when, and why? How can we understand life? How can we be all we should be? Softly through the years comes a quiet answer: "I just love the Lord," Hulda said.

One special thing we learned from Velda was how to make tostadas. She knew how to make them, of course, long before our town could boast of five or more Mexican restaurants. The thing that made Velda's tostadas great was the addition of peas, green peas. Velda is gone now, and I do not know if she learned to add peas when she spent time in Mexico, if she heard the idea from a friend, or if she dreamed it up herself. I only know that after we ate tostadas at Velda's house, we never ate them without peas again. Try it. It's a Pie Lady thing, definitely, the perfect thing to serve with lemony iced tea on a hundred-degree summer day.

Just love the Lord.

TOSTADAS

> 12 tostada shells
> Pinto beans, cooked, fried, and mashed
> 2 pounds ground beef, cooked and salted
> Cooked peas
> Lettuce, chopped
> Grated cheese
> Sour cream
> Chili sauce

Beginning with the tostada shell on the plate, add in this order: beans, ground beef, peas, lettuce, and cheese. Top with sour cream and chili sauce.

30

Singing the Cake

THE KANSAS FAMILY

For thou, Lord, only makest me dwell in safety.

—PSALM 4:8

THEY LIVED IN a Kansas farmhouse, all nine of them, seven children with their mom and dad. The dad worked in a factory, days. He worked in his orchard, with his sheep, or remodeling the house, evenings. He answered questions, read books out loud, and taught each of his four daughters to change a tire. He was the one who checked the windows when a thunderstorm threatened.

Because thunderstorms did roll across the plains. When the wind blew dust and rain against the house, stinging or pounding, you definitely wanted the windows closed.

And tires did go flat. That is the hazard of driving down a dirt road to a tall white farmhouse. Oh yes, life on a farm, complete with an orchard and a flock of sheep—it's best if you know how to change a tire, getting there.

This Kansas farmhouse was the place where the mother cooked and cleaned and sewed, where she grew flowers and a vegetable garden, and taught the children how to work. She baked thousands of cookies, loaves of bread, and cinnamon rolls, with the four daughters right there beside her, grabbing the ends and watching just how it was done.

The children planned and played, gorgeous messes of play dough and blanket tents. They tramped through the woods, swam in the muddy Twin Ponds, sledded down the hills. They fed kittens and baby lambs. They warmed their jammies on the woodstove, cold winter evenings, while the wind whirled and pounded at the windows that were fastened up tight.

When it came around to Sunday, the mother made a big spread. Even without company, they were nine around the table! She usually topped off the meal with a cobbler or a crisp. It was always the same, the children thought. A cobbler again, or a crisp. A crisp or a cobbler.

One day the mother visited an aunt's house and came home with a new recipe for cake. The family cheered and left the cobblers behind. Many Sundays after that, one of the daughters mixed up the cake while another stirred up the topping. The only problem was that this cake took lots of watching. Once or twice the frosting burned black under the broiler.

So the children made up a song, and as long as the frosting was in the broiler, they sang to the tune of "Waltzing Matilda": "Cake in the oven, cake in the oven, cake in the oven . . ." and no one forgot the cake.

The girls mixed it and baked it. The whole family ate it. Sometimes the boys even let the cake server slip so that they grabbed two pieces instead of one.

It was perfect, it was sweet, and they did it Sunday after Sunday, year after year. Over time, even in-laws who thought they were coconut haters decided it was perfect. They loved the farmhouse and the orchard too, you know. And they knew how to change a tire, how to fasten up the windows before a storm.

You can make this cake too—or maybe you can get one of your own small boys or girls to mix it up. You can even see if they will sing while the topping bubbles and broils. Maybe they will think of singing other times—busy times, anxious times, I-can-hardly-do-this times.

Maybe you live out on a rocky, hilly farm, in an old, old house. Maybe you not only close the windows before a storm— you have to turn up the heat in the living room and close the upstairs doors. Well. You can sing while the broiler's on, and you can set the cake on the table with a grand flourish. You can serve it, warm and perfect, and you can maybe let the cake server slip under a second piece.

Some days are just plain good.

OUR FAMILY'S FAVORITE CAKE

Cake
   1 standard size Duncan Hines Butter Golden Cake Mix

Broiled topping
   6 tablespoons butter, softened
   1 cup brown sugar
   1½ cup shredded coconut
   4½ tablespoons milk

Bake in a 10 x 15-inch sheet cake pan at 350°F for 20 minutes, or until a few little crumbs cling to a toothpick that is poked into the cake.

Make topping: Mix softened butter, brown sugar, coconut, and milk. Spread carefully on hot cake. Broil until bubbly and slightly brown. Watch carefully! You do want it brown, but it can burn easily.

This is scrumptious eaten warm out of the oven.

31

The Jelly Lady and the Meat Loaf Man

DELORES

For thou shalt eat the labour of thine hands: happy shalt thou be.

—PSALM 128:2

DEEDEE SAT AT the table, her chin in her hands, watching her mother slice crabapples into the big jelly pot. DeeDee liked the way the little apples sat in Mom's large hands, liked the way the knife flew through them, down and around, liked the tangy apple smell in the air.

DeeDee watched Mom pick over the chokecherries, watched her turn the faucet on and rinse the dark red fruit. DeeDee watched Mom turn the faucet on and let water stream slowly into the kettle, just enough water to barely cover. She watched her slowly stir with the wooden jelly spoon. Mom poked at the fruit, called it soft, and set the strainer over a large pan. She got out the special jelly cloth and set it in the strainer and then carefully poured in the cherries with their juice. The cloth soaked up the juice and turned a dark purple-red. The kitchen filled up with a purple, earthy, end-of-summer smell.

Mom was making jelly. Or rather, Mom was making juice so she could make jelly. Over and over, DeeDee watched Mom do that. Over and over, she watched Mom pour the hot jelly into jars, she watched her load up boxes of jars to take to the farmers' market.

Mom's customers loved the bread she made, they loved the jelly, and they loved to stop at Mom's table and buy bread and jelly and pies. Once a family came and bought a bag of buns and a jar of jelly. They went to their car by the curb with their find. In a few minutes, they came back with money for another bag of buns. In a few minutes more, they brought a pile of coins for the third bag.

Mom was pleased, but DeeDee was not surprised. The jelly was perfect. The buns were perfect. Mom was the Jelly Lady, and of course she was the Pie Queen. DeeDee loved to watch Mom make things, and she loved to help where she could. She helped pick and wash chokecherries. She helped stir the jelly pot. She washed stacks of dishes and carried jars. Good things happened in that kitchen: cinnamon rolls every week, round white buns, a cup of hot chocolate for the men working late at night. Mom made them all with her own capable hands. Mom knew what she was doing.

And it wasn't just Mom.

Some days when Mom was away from home or maybe extra busy, DeeDee watched her dad working at the kitchen table.

Dad liked doing it, DeeDee decided. His thick, strong fingers took a loaf of bread from the bin and pulled it apart into uniform chunks. Yum, it smelled like bread. DeeDee watched the crumbs grow into a mountain of bread in the white bowl. Piles of onion sizzled in butter in the cast iron pan on the stove. Dad watched the onions, stirred them, and finally dumped them over the bread. He sprinkled it all with seasoning, poured in streams of broth and milk, and topped it with an egg. Stir, taste, sprinkle. Add a little salt.

"Oh ho," Dad said while DeeDee smiled to herself. "Ooh, that's gonna taste good." He piled the bread onto the shredded poultry in the roaster and settled on the lid. Then he set the roaster in the oven to bake. It looked like fun, DeeDee thought, almost as fun as meat loaf mornings.

Meat loaf mornings, which were busy Sunday mornings, Dad dumped together ground beef (maybe a little ground pork mixed in, if he wanted to), tomato juice and milk and egg, seasonings and chunks of bread. He mixed the meat loaf with his hands, packed it into the greased glass pan, and spread the spicy topping over the top. The meat loaf baked while the family was in church, and they all loved to walk in the door afterward.

"Oh," Dad would say. "Ooh, this smells good. I think we're going to stay here for dinner."

DeeDee loved watching her dad make that meat loaf. She could see that making things with your hands was good work. It had to be fun, working in the kitchen.

Day after day, DeeDee helped stir jelly and wash dishes. She helped her mom make hot chocolate to serve the men after a long day out in the harvest field. She helped to sell the bread and jelly and pies at the farmers' market. She learned from her mom as she worked: it's worth the time, the extra effort, the job well done.

DeeDee listened to her dad tell of his "baching" years. Stock your kitchen with bread, corn, potatoes, butter, onions, garlic sausage, and *griewe* (cracklings), he said. Stock your stove with a cast iron pan. It doesn't take much to keep yourself fed, DeeDee learned from her dad.

DeeDee grew up—known as Delores now, she is still DeeDee to her friends. She was far away from home, in a country where children ran up to her gate with their bruises and cuts, asking for help, when she realized the truth of the promise: if you leave houses and lands and family, God will bless you with home and family, heaped up and running over. Her friends there invited her into their kitchens, showed her how to cook with one pot and one spoon. They asked her to stir the sauce for them and made her feel at home. Life was full of blessings, DeeDee thought, too many blessings to hold in your hands.

DeeDee moved back home, and finally moved to her own house miles away. She took a real Pie Lady job cooking in the local café. There, back in the kitchen, she stirs up comfort with her hands, sets chili on the stove to cook on a snowy day. Life is good; blessings overflow her hands as she measures and stirs and remembers. It's worth the time, she learned from her mom long ago. Share what you have, she learned from her friends far away. Once she read in a magazine that a test kitchen found out that to get full-flavored meat loaf, you need to add dairy. DeeDee smiled. She had already learned that from her dad.

Love by doing.

PETER'S MEAT LOAF

1½ pound ground beef
1½ cup torn bread pieces
1 medium onion, chopped
1 egg
½ cup milk
1 cup tomato juice
1 teaspoon salt
Pepper, as desired

Topping

¼ cup ketchup
¼ teaspoon ground nutmeg
1 teaspoon dry mustard
3 tablespoons brown sugar

Preheat oven to 350°F. Combine all meat loaf ingredients and mix well with your hands. Pack into an 8 x 12-inch pan or a 2-quart glass baking dish. Mix together topping ingredients and spread over the meat loaf. Bake 1½ hour.

PETER'S STUFFING

1 loaf bread
1 teaspoon ground sage
½ teaspoon poultry seasoning
1½ teaspoon salt
½ teaspoon pepper
½ cup or more butter
2 large onions, chopped
2 cups milk or broth
1 egg, beaten

Slice the loaf of bread and tear it into small, uniform pieces. Toss with sage, poultry seasoning, salt, and pepper.

Melt butter in a heavy skillet (cast iron if you have it). Add onions and stir until they are soft. Pour milk or broth and egg over the bread crumbs and toss together. Add onions and butter. Add additional salt and pepper as desired.

Pile on top of sliced baked chicken or turkey and cover. Bake for 1 hour at 350°F, or 2 hours at 300°F. Uncover for the last 15 or 20 minutes to lightly brown the stuffing.

IRIS'S BESTSELLING CHOKECHERRY CRABAPPLE JELLY

2 cups chokecherry juice*
2 cups crabapple juice*
4 cups granulated sugar
Butter

No pectin is needed in this recipe, because the apples have enough. Set a small bowl in the freezer to chill. Stir juices and sugar together into a big pot. Bring to a boil, stirring with the stained wooden jelly spoon. Cook and stir for several minutes, adding a small spoonful of butter to keep the foam down. After the right amount of time (about 15 minutes), start dripping little pools into the cold bowl and see how it sets up. When it's the right thickness (just as thick or as thin as you like it), ladle into warm jars and screw on the lids that are being kept warm in a pot of hot water with a touch of vinegar. Then you can store your jelly in the fridge for several weeks.

If you want to keep it longer than that, you will need to seal the jars in a hot water bath according to canning directions. (Iris always just made sure the jars and the jelly were hot and that the lids sealed.)

*To make juice: Cover washed chokecherries (the ones you handpicked yourself) with water and cook for a minimum of 20 minutes, until very soft. Strain through a jelly cloth. Do the same with cut-up crabapples from the tree in the yard.

32

Love, Mom

JEWEL AND LAVAUNA

By love serve one another.

—GALATIANS 5:13

BIRTHDAYS WERE A big deal at our house, great big family events. It started off with a birthday breakfast, the breakfast of our choice. Mom put candles in the pancakes (or whatever breakfast food we had chosen), and then we opened our gift. When we turned thirteen, Mom said we were old enough now that we didn't need to just "take" on our birthday. Sometime that day we needed to do something kind for someone else. And then we topped the day off with a birthday supper, with something on the menu that Mom knew we loved.

The year I turned eighteen, my birthday fell on a Friday. When it got close we all realized that was the evening we were expecting out-of-state guests. These weren't guests we knew very well; in fact, they were two visiting preachers who had come to our area to hold a set of revival meetings. Oh no.

We really didn't feel up to the normal candle-blowing demonstrations in front of the revival ministers. Oh dear. This would definitely put a block in our birthday celebration. Because we couldn't have a birthday party without, well, mentioning the birthday, without candles and everything. I did not want to do all that with the preachers there.

Oh well. What is one less party? That is just how life works sometimes.

The day before my birthday, I dragged slowly into the house. It had been a long day, and I was glad it was over. But something was up, I could see it right away. The house shone, and the table was set for a party, an hour or two ahead. When I sank into a chair, glad to be home, I noticed the slow cooker and smelled pepper steak, my favorite thing.

"I thought we'd just celebrate early," Mom said. She was smiling. And then I saw the marionberry pie, grand and warm on the cleaned-off counter of a tidy house. Right then, there was nothing I loved better than a tidy house, though you can guarantee I always dreaded helping to tidy it. There was nothing that gleamed better than the wiped-off kitchen counters, nothing sweeter than my very own favorite pie.

That birthday dinner sparkled with surprise. I've never forgotten the grandeur of my favorite pie on a night that was not even my birthday. It was so special, so thoughtful, so Mom.

Before we were old enough to cook, Mom taught my sisters and me to make mud pies. She showed us how to mix the dirt and water, how to dump it into a pan and bake it in the sun. We spent whole summers playing house after that. We made flatbread on a margarine lid and stirred with mud into grass clippings to make roast beef. We made shingle bacon and rocky chicken casserole. We swept our floors and shook our rugs and arranged our dishes.

Mom did a lot of cooking, and we were not very old when she taught us how to cook. We started out by turning the drips of pancake batter, teeny-tiny pancakes. Then we learned to make scrambled eggs and brownies and chocolate chip cookies, baked fluffy rice and chocolate cake with sauce. I remember how much fun it was to choose something to make and then to make it all by myself, without any help. I didn't even want to tell what it was that I was making.

Mom made corn-putting-up day an event, something we waited for. We each had our own special job that we half suspected no one else could do. One of us was best at cutting corn off the cob. Two of us boiled the corn and cooled it. We had old blankets on the floor to catch the corn that dropped. We had cleaned everything off the counter before we started in. At the end of the day each bag was flat and neat and carefully marked and the corn was in the freezer.

We also learned how to have an Evening. It was a big deal to have everything tidy, everything done, everyone home. Dad would read aloud, or we would sing, or talk, or get out an icy drink. You never have enough of those evenings— you spend the time and effort, and they pay. You sit down and realize why you folded the wash in the afternoon, why you rushed around vacuuming, why you did the dishes although you really did not feel like it. It's the very best part of a tidy house: a special hour, an event that counts up the good times.

When sorrow comes, and one of the family goes to heaven ahead of the rest, you are glad for every birthday breakfast, for every special job, for every family evening. Life flies by—we have to grab a moment, shine it up, and make the most of it.

It's funny how those glittery moments are the ones you remember best. We hoed out buckets of stickery weeds, swept out Dad's shop every week, and tidied the house countless times. But when I think back, I remember sitting on the lawn under the water cooler that was settled onto the windowsill, having a picnic in the shade of the house. I remember Mom getting us three black-and-white kittens. I remember laughing without stopping, and a filled-up, beautiful table. That extra glitter on ordinary days makes childhood a gift to keep forever.

I was only eighteen when I married Matt and moved thirteen miles down the road. I started in cleaning and cooking and gardening, taking time to read and walk and dream. I would cook big meals, have huge messes to clean up, and feel too tired to clean them. I neglected the dusting and forgot to do laundry. I planted a garden and neglected the weeds.

Harvesttime came around with regularity. Harvesttime means long hours out in the field. It means drastic fall weather, cold or hot, back and forth and back again. It means wind blowing dust in your eyes and ripping the foil off casserole pans. It means black bugs when there is no wind, crawling over the cookies and into your tea. It means schedules and lunch boxes and hurrying and waiting. And for me, it means cooking with Matt's mom.

Mom and I have cooked together at corn harvest for over twenty years now, and we know what to expect. I know her silverware, her tea, and the ice she uses, the hot cupcakes she brings out, the cherry crisp, the fried chicken and the stew and the cinnamon rolls.

She never forgets the plates or the cups, as I occasionally do. The food is hot, on time, and she takes the time to park at a good place to block the wind.

We've eaten lots of other meals with Matt's family. We've had Sunday dinners when the roast is sliced just so, the corn seasoned perfectly, the lettuce shredded fine, and the chocolate cake fresh with shiny frosting. We've had Christmas dinners with special meat and plates of homemade fudge. We've had snacks in the evening with popcorn and no-bakes and pop. And the children pop the popcorn themselves in the microwave that sits low enough for them to reach, and we make coffee and pass the candy around and talk, with the table stretched out wall to wall, family and friends in every available space. We go up and down and around in our discussions, opinions flying, good times rolling.

But when I think back over twenty years, think of Mom, think of cooking, I think of harvest.

Harvesttime isn't easy. There are so many schedules, so many deadlines to meet. I cook up a bunch of food and leave a messy kitchen while I dash out to the field, two minutes late. "I can't do this," I chant to myself as I drive.

But I get to the field and Mom is positioning her vehicle just right, blocking the wind. She has food ready too (we each do a part). She has her basket of silverware, her plates, her chairs, the sack for trash when we are done.

And Grandma talks to the children, and the men talk about the harvest, and even in the middle of a long and busy day, we sit for a few minutes, all together. We pass the cupcakes around the circle before we are up and off to work again.

And a killdeer calls, and the smallest child runs off, scuffing up dust. He plays in the corn and tries to decide who he wants to ride with.

It's a very short time, and the combines are rolling again, and we ride in on the truck or meander home the long way around, thinking of the dishes on the counter. Or maybe we just drive over to Mom's house and sit in her living room drinking pop and reading the newspaper.

I will give you Matt's mom's recipe for gingerbread—it's a recipe she adjusted just right and gave me many years ago—and my own mom's recipe for marionberry pie. Marionberries are a type of blackberry, a little redder than and not quite as seedy as other blackberries. If you can find marionberries, great. If you can't, you can use other blackberries, though it will be a slightly seedier experience. Or go to the grocery store and buy the frozen triple berry mix, which includes marionberries. One bag will make two pies.

And gingerbread is one of the best fall desserts. I bake it in a small cake pan and serve it warm with lots of soft whipped cream. I make it instead of birthday cakes sometimes. I've made it for tea parties, and once in a while we even take it out to the harvest field.

The harvest days will soon be gone and winter will be here. It's only now, a few weeks at the most, that we work together and cook together and try to match schedules and deadlines. They're long days full of hurry. But it's the potato salad and the fried chicken, the talks we had and the time we shared, that we remember.

I take a deep breath and serve the food and sit down under the sky. The time we spend, that Pie Lady rush, the planning and the hurrying we did—it all pays off. We'll never regret the times we shared. We pull out camping chairs, we set up the food on a tailgate, and out under the wide blue sky we bow for prayer.

God is good.

GINGERBREAD

  1 cup flour
  ½ cup granulated sugar
  ½ teaspoon salt
  ¼ teaspoon ground nutmeg
  ¼ teaspoon ground cloves
  ¼ teaspoon ground allspice
  ½ teaspoon ground cinnamon
  1 teaspoon ground ginger
  ½ teaspoon baking powder
  ⅓ cup shortening
  ½ cup molasses
  ½ cup warm water
  ¼ cup additional water
  1 teaspoon baking soda
  1 egg

Heat oven to 350°F. Stir flour, sugar, salt, nutmeg, cloves, allspice, cinnamon, ginger, and baking powder together in a mixing bowl. Add shortening, molasses, and warm water. Beat 2 minutes. Pour ¼ cup additional water in a microwaveable mug and heat until it boils. Stir in baking soda and add to the mixture in the mixing bowl. Beat for a few seconds. Add egg. Beat 1 minute. Turn into greased and floured 8 x 8-inch pan or a round 9-inch cake pan. (Matt's mom made it in a tin 8 x 8-inch pan, and served it with lots of soft, sweet whipped cream. I sometimes bake it in a

round cake pan and cut it like a pie, but just like she did,
I always serve it with big heaps of real whipped cream.)
Bake for 35–45 minutes, or until just a few crumbs cling to
a toothpick that you poke into the center.

MARIONBERRY PIE

Crust for (9-inch) two-crust pie
1½ pound frozen marionberries (enough to fill a 4 cup
measure heaping full)
1 rounded cup granulated sugar, plus more for topping
crust
2½ tablespoons tapioca
Pinch salt

Heat oven to 350°F. Roll out pie crusts and place bottom
crust in pie pan. In a large mixing bowl, combine marionberries, 1 rounded cup sugar, tapioca, and salt. Stir slightly
and allow berries to thaw for 1 or 2 minutes. Stir lightly
until the sugar coats the berries completely. Pile into pie
shell and rub a little water along the edges of the pie shell.
Cut design into top crust and place it over the pie. Crimp
edges to seal. Sprinkle with 1 or 2 tablespoons additional sugar, and cover edges of pastry with foil. Bake for
45 minutes. Remove foil, and continue baking until hot and
bubbly, 15 minutes or more.

THE AUTHOR

Greta Isaac is a Mennonite writer and homemaker who lives on a farm in Kansas with her husband, Matt, and their four children. She writes for her friends and her family, and occasionally for *Purpose* and other magazines. Isaac and her family are members of a Mennonite church near their home.